D0732563

CAMPUS
CONFIDENTIAL

CALGARY PUBLIC LIBRARY

OCT   2011

CAMPUS CONFIDENTIAL

100 startling things you don't know about Canadian universities

Ken S. Coates
Bill Morrison

James Lorimer & Company Ltd., Publishers
Toronto

Copyright © 2011 by Ken S.Coates and Bill Morrison

All rights reserved. No part of this book may be reproduced or transmitted in any form or by any means, electronic or mechanical, including photocopying, or by any information storage or retrieval system, without permission in writing from the publisher.

James Lorimer & Company Ltd., Publishers acknowledges the support of the Ontario Arts Council. We acknowledge the financial support of the Government of Canada through the Canada Book Fund for our publishing activities. We acknowledge the support of the Canada Council for the Arts which last year invested $20.1 million in writing and publishing throughout Canada. We acknowledge the Government of Ontario through the Ontario Media Development Corporation's Ontario Book Initiative.

 **Canada Council
for the Arts**   **Conseil des Arts
du Canada**

ONTARIO ARTS COUNCIL
CONSEIL DES ARTS DE L'ONTARIO

Library and Archives Canada Cataloguing in Publication

Coates, Kenneth, 1956-
        Campus confidential : 100 startling things you didn't know about Canadian universities / by Ken S. Coates, Bill Morrison.

Includes index.
Issued also in electronic format.
ISBN 978-1-55277-650-6

        1. Universities and colleges--Canada. 2. Education, Higher--Canada.
I. Morrison, William R. (William Robert), 1942- II. Title.

LB2329.8.C2C63 2011   378.71   C2010-907794-6

James Lorimer & Company Ltd., Publishers
317 Adelaide Street West, Suite 1002
Toronto, ON, Canada
M5V 1P9
www.lorimer.ca

Printed and bound in Canada

For William, Spencer, and Katie
For Graeme, Ella, James, Henry, and Quinn
In the hope that the universities that await them will be up to the
challenge of the 21st century.

Contents

IV. Do Canadian Universities Work? 83

V. The View from the Front of the Class 101

VI. A Professor's Life 131

VII. Universities in Canadian Society 161

VIII. Are Canada's Universities Ready for the Twenty-First Century? 205

Epilogue: Preparing Canada's Universities for the Challenges Ahead 229

Sources 239

Introduction

Universities are supposed to provide answers to the big questions in life—but they have generated many questions of their own. Does our university system work? Are employers happy with the graduates? Why might some universities have to close? Are students well served by their teachers and institutions, and do they work hard at their studies? Does academic research really fuel national prosperity? Do universities give good value for money? (They cost vast sums to operate. The current operating budget of the University of Toronto is $1.6 billion—more than that of the province of Prince Edward Island.)

Who really pays for the cost of an undergraduate education? How are Canadian universities doing by international standards? Why are there so many universities, and should students really be studying on-line? What do faculty members do in the summer, and are their salaries reasonable? Why are low university tuition rates one of the major financial benefits given to wealthy Canadians? Are corporations driving academic agendas at Canadian universities?

These and dozens of other questions have troubled us for years. We have wondered why there was not more discussion about these issues, which should matter to people well beyond the campus boundaries.

Universities play an important, but largely unexamined, role in our communities and our country. Academics don't like it when outsiders critique their operations, but since universities operate on public money, they are not, and should not be, free from scrutiny and criticism. Some of it can be pretty nasty: the now-defunct *Frank* magazine used to publish a column called "The Groves of Academe," which poked cruel fun at the foibles of academics, and there is much anxiety on campus when the *Globe and Mail's* Margaret Wente turns her witty but acerbic pen to matters scholarly. In United States bookstores, there are shelves full of volumes decrying the absurdities and failings of universities and colleges.

Canadians, in contrast, are much more quiet, polite, and calm about discussing their university system—perhaps too much so. *Campus Confidential* is intended to be provocative and informative. We want Canadians to think deeply about the nature of the university and the choices we must make in the coming years about the system's future. Consider this book a conversation starter.

We do not hate universities and this is not an exposé. Rather, we care deeply about them. We don't come to praise higher education, nor to bury it, but to suggest ways it can be improved. Canadian universities are not in crisis—yet. But we do think there are some major and worrying forces at play. We'd like to see the system prepare for them instead of being blindsided by them. We believe we have one of the best university systems in the world, but we also think it could be made a good deal better.

Next to health care, education is the largest sector of our economy, and universities consume a large percentage of the education spending. Despite this, people know surprisingly little about how universities actually work. This isn't a pitch for huge new infusions of public money either. We argue that the money in the system could be spent more intelligently and to greater effect.

We hate to hear the phrase "it's only academic." It suggests we spend our time in esoteric and irrelevant pursuits. We decided to write a practical, not an "ivory tower" book. We wanted to get straight to the point, without providing masses of examples and piles of evidence—as academics properly and expertly do most of the time. We offer observations and ideas derived from many years of studying and working in universities. The hundred short chapters that make up this book deal with issues vital to young people thinking about university, to students already in university, to faculty coping with increasing demands on their time and abilities, administrators trying to achieve the best results on a limited budget, and to the general public wondering what goes on behind the greenery on those ivy-covered walls—in short, just about everybody.

We are a disparate pair. One of us was born in Ontario, the other in Alberta. Bill started university in 1959, spent all but two of the following fifty-one years as student, teacher, and administrator, and retired, as Professor Emeritus, in 2010. Ken started his studies in 1974 and, save for one year in Japan and one in Vancouver, has been in the system continuously since then. We've studied and worked at the following institutions as teachers and administrators: McMaster, Western Ontario, Toronto, Queen's,

British Columbia, Manitoba, Brandon, Victoria, Northern British Columbia, Lakehead, Quest, New Brunswick (Saint John), Saskatchewan, and Waterloo in Canada, Waikato in New Zealand, and Florida State and Duke in the United States. It sounds rather as if we can't hold down a job, but remember that this list covers nearly ninety years between the two of us!

We have engaged in discussions over the years with many of our colleagues and professional friends about the shape and nature of our university system, and asked some of them to review this book for mistakes and oversights, but the ideas (and the errors) remain ours. We particularly want to thank Kelley Teahen, Rick Miner, James Barnett, Ernie Barber, Bill Chesney, Mark Evered, Sean Van Koughnett, Bud Walker, James Skidmore, Tobi Day-Hamilton, Feridun Hamdullahpur, Tim Kenyon, David Docherty, Tara Collington, Greg Poelzer, Emanuel Carvalho, Robert W. Park, Bruce Muirhead, Lynne Jelokhani-Niaraki, Paul Doherty, Dave Hannah, Michael Atkinson, Kelly Saretsky, Meg Beckel, Chris Read, Clive Keen, and Keith Taylor.

Universities are enormously important to the economic and social health of Canada. If the country is to continue to prosper throughout the lives of our children and grandchildren, universities have to prosper too, although perhaps not in their current form. Canada needs an open and aggressive debate about the role and purpose of universities, about the activities of students and faculty, and about the multi-billion dollar expenditures made with the firm—but largely uncontested—assumption that this investment will make Canada better and more prosperous. The ideas in *Campus Confidential* have been bubbling for a long time, and we know that many Canadians want to know a great deal more about universities. We hope you find this book a good place to start.

Ken S. Coates, BA, MA, PhD, Dean of Arts, University of Waterloo
Bill Morrison, BA, MA, PhD, DLit (Hon.), Professor Emeritus of History,
University of Northern British Columbia

I

A Student's Guide to University

University Isn't for Everyone

So you want to go to university. Good for you. For thousands of Canadians, it's a fine choice. As you think about it, though, let us offer you a few words of friendly advice.

First, ask yourself this question: why do you want to go? Is it because your parents want you to, because you are really interested in what university has to offer, because your friends are going, because you can't think of anything else to do, because you want the secure career that a university degree promises, because the idea of learning about the world fascinates you, because you'd like to learn a skill that you could use to help humankind? All of the above? None of them?

It's important to know why you are going. Not everyone who starts university finishes it. At some places the drop-out rate approaches 50 per cent—nearly half the people who start, don't get a degree. Some quit, some flunk, others go elsewhere. Sometimes it's because they find it too difficult, and other times they decide it's not for them. The drop-out rate is much lower in professional programs, and overall nationally, it's about 15 per cent, or one in seven.

Ask yourself another question: do I like to read? Not Harlequin Romances or *The Da Vinci Code*, but books about the world. Do you read a newspaper, either in print or on-line? Are you interested in politics, the Hubble Space Telescope, foreign countries, Shakespeare, the Large Hadron Collider, the Roman Empire? That's what university is about. If you are rolling your eyes, well...

Do you have the necessary skills? It can be hard to tell. High school grades are no longer a reliable indication. You may have graduated with 75 per cent, which was a very good result two generations ago, but nowadays it won't get you into a prestigious place. The median at McGill for incoming students in 2009 was 90 or 92 per cent, depending on the province you came from. There are plenty of places that will take you at 75 per cent or less, but you may have to relocate.

Is there something you'd rather do first? Travel perhaps, join the work-force, or do volunteer work? It won't hurt to wait a year or two—the universities will still be there, and you'll have a better idea of what you want. Don't wait too long though.

Would you rather work in a field that doesn't require a degree? Perhaps the skilled trades? You can make just as much money, start making it earlier, do what you really want to do—not what someone else thinks you should do—by going to a technical institution.

If you decide not to go right away, or ever, you've not necessarily made a bad choice. University isn't for everyone. If, on the other hand, you decide that it's for you, then you have our best wishes. Good luck!

Which University You Attend Matters Less Than You Think

Your choice depends a great deal on what you plan to study. All universities in Canada consider themselves above average, and all of them try (or say they try) to achieve excellence in both teaching and research. The public—and importantly employers—have bought this idea, which for some disciplines is true.

But in fact a degree in history, political science, environmental science, and a number of other disciplines is just as good from one place as another. If you are planning to be a teacher, a civil servant, or get any kind of non-professional job, any university will do, since most employers usually don't care where you got your degree.

It's different for specialized programs such as law and business, and for students planning to go to graduate school. There's a strong perception that some law schools are better than others—or at least more prestigious—and getting into a top one helps a law graduate get into a good law firm. The same is true of business schools. Getting into graduate school means getting good grades from a well-regarded university, one that has a good reputation among academics in that discipline. It also means being able to get letters of reference from well-known scholars. A letter from Carl Weiman, the Nobel-prize-winning physicist who came to UBC in 2006 is going to carry far more weight than one from Professor X, a physicist at Nowhere U.

The *Maclean's* ratings aren't much help, because they rate universities as a whole (though they do rank professional schools separately). The University of Toronto and McGill may top the big university category, but it doesn't mean all their programs are the best. You have to do your own research, and in particular talk to faculty members you trust.

But for students not headed to the professions or graduate school, it really doesn't matter, so you can choose a school based on other considerations: location, climate, or party reputation. If you want a degree that will make employers take notice, though, you'll probably have to study outside the country.

There's Nothing Wrong with the Skilled Trades

Doug installs high-end kitchens for a living, and he is doing very well. He's smart, talented, and very good at running his own company. By all measures, he's a classic example of the fulfilling careers available to those in the skilled trades.

Doug also has a university degree. He went to university because his parents expected it, many of his friends were going, and because his high school teachers pointed him in that direction. He loved working with his hands and had a strong mix of entrepreneurship, creativity, and technical proficiency. But he bought the university propaganda and came under the spell of the counsellor's mantra: go to university, get a degree, aspire to a white-collar career.

He slogged through his BA degree, doing as little as possible to get a C-average. He never really warmed to his academic discipline, though he did party a lot. He worked with a carpenter in his spare time and in the summer to pay the bills and clearly loved this work more than book learning. He graduated because he was expected to, but he had no interest in pursuing a career related to his studies.

Doug shows up statistically as a university success story. Universities would claim that his studies gave him a greater appreciation of the world and even made him more successful at his chosen trades and business career. You could also argue that university was a waste of money for both him and the government and that he should have been given more encouragement to consider a trades career from the beginning. Doug viewed university as an extension of high school, as something smart kids were just expected to do. He bears no grudge against the university he attended—he had fun there out of class—but he doesn't see the place as critical to his subsequent success.

Mark is a somewhat different case. He was an academic superstar in high school, with stratospheric grades in math and science. He had his choice of the best universities in Canada and received big scholarships. He completed his MSc and then his PhD at a prestigious institution. He married a fellow scientist and seemed destined for a fine scholarly career. But the passion was gone. He no longer found pleasure in scientific discovery and realized he did not want to be an academic. Now in his late twenties, he had no plans for what to do next, and he had no other marketable skills.

Then Mark, like Doug, discovered he loved working with his hands and had a gift for woodwork. With no regrets, he stepped away from the academy and began a career making high-quality furniture.

Doug and Mark's experience, and that of thousands like them, shows that universities are not for everyone, not even for every intelligent young person. The idea that people with brains must get degrees—and that people with no degrees have no brains—is appallingly wrong and unfair.

The lesson here is that the trades should be given equal billing with university education in high school. Students should be encouraged to follow their passions, capitalize on their abilities, and find a career that brings satisfaction—and a decent income. Universities are too often presented as the best—if not the only—option for bright students. This is bad for the students, and for the economic health of Canada.

University Tuition Is a Bargain

Is a university education a private good, a public one, or a combination of the two? Is it a solid investment in students' futures, or is it an investment by the state, designed to increase the nation's productivity, competitiveness, and general well-being, and therefore a shared or common good? If it's the first, it seems fair that students (and their parents) should pay the lion's share of the cost of a university education. If it's the second, then the state and taxpayers should pay much of the cost. Which is it?

This question is a matter of endless debate, with governments and universities raising fees as much as they dare, while the Canadian Federation of Students and the New Democratic Party look longingly at European countries, where university is free, and demand that fees be lowered (forgetting that these systems have much less accessibility). Canadian provinces, except Quebec, have wavered between tuition freezes and moderate increases, while permitting much higher fees for career-focused programs such as MBAs and law. In the 1970s tuition fees covered about 20 per cent of the cost of running the universities. In 2008 they covered 50 per cent—a sharp rise that allegedly contains a substantial government subsidy for student participation.

Attending university can be quite expensive. The cost of tuition alone for a standard BA degree ranges from a low of $1,800 a year (two semesters) in Quebec to a high of $6,700 in Nova Scotia. But these numbers pale in comparison with the costs at elite American private schools, where tuition fees plus room and board in the region of $50,000 a year are standard. Specialized programs—medicine, law, or the MBAs offered at the top Canadian universities—can cost between $20,000 and $35,000 for a year's tuition, but relatively few students enter these programs.

Various kinds of financial support are available, ranging from entrance scholarships and bursaries to institutional and provincial government loans (the latter's student loan programs being heavily underwritten by the federal government). And more than half of all students work part time, on or off-campus, while attending university. Summer jobs—and for those enrolled in special programs, co-operative education placements—allow students to learn and earn at the same time. And for anyone still short, banks and other financial institutions are ready with loans as well. There is also funding for special groups: First Nations students, for instance, are often funded by their bands, and there is also some funding available for the children of veterans, students with disabilities, and others. One difference between Canada and the United States, however, is that we do not offer nearly as much by way of athletic scholarships.

With all this support available, half of all students graduate from university without any debt. For the other half, the average debt now exceeds $25,000—a large but hardly crippling sum for someone with good lifetime career prospects. Universities worry about the amount of outside work students feel compelled to accept during the university year because jobs of more than ten hours per week can harm academic performance. But it's also clear that many students work for reasons of lifestyle as much as necessity—to cover the cost of meals, drinks, cars, movies, and electronic gadgets.

The standard theory of supply and demand suggests that higher prices should drive down enrolment. In general, this does not appear to be the case. In fact, students fight to get into the really expensive programs like law and the MBA. If a university degree is half a private benefit and half a public good, and if students pay for about half the cost of their education, the fee structure would seem just about right. The real unfairness (see Chapter 17) is that the Canadian structure makes these fees cheaper for the rich than for the poor.

5 No One Agrees on What Students Should Know

Fifty years ago universities generally accepted that "every educated man (shudder!)" would know certain things. All students, regardless of program, studied a foreign language (French counted as "foreign"); arts students took a science course specially designed for them, and science students took English. At the graduate level there were similar requirements. A generation ago, PhD students had to demonstrate competence in not one, but two foreign languages (again counting French as foreign). The rationale for scientists was that a great deal of scientific research was published in, for instance, German. Historians needed to read the language of their particular field: Latin, or whatever.

What lay behind these requirements was the belief that there was a common body of knowledge that marked an educated person. Whether students agreed or not was irrelevant. That was the way things were, and at many places there were other compulsory courses: religion, physical education, philosophy, or psychology.

Most of this began to crumble in the late 1960s, when students' wishes began to be taken into account. They wanted to study what was "relevant" to them, not what some university committee thought they ought to know. The language requirement was dropped for undergraduates, and eventually at most places there were hardly any compulsory courses at all, except for English. Of course, if you are a sociology major, you have to take certain sociology courses, but otherwise you can choose what you please.

Debate about this issue has never died, and many universities have tried different ways to broaden students' experiences into disciplines they might not have chosen voluntarily. The University of Manitoba is currently doing interesting things in the area. At some places there is a "breadth requirement" that requires students to take at least one course from lists of physical and natural sciences, and from humanities and social sciences. Other universities have "core" or "foundation" courses that all students are required to take. There is talk of adopting the American liberal-arts model that has all students taking exactly the same courses in their first year (the University of King's College in Halifax does this), with Great Books and Great Ideas as a prominent feature.

This issue will never be resolved, because at its heart lies a simple question: should students study what they want to study, or what universities think they ought to study? The question is easier to answer in the sciences, since there's consensus on what a physicist, a physician, or a mathematician needs to know—though less agreement on whether they should also take a course in English literature. In the arts and social sciences, however, there's very little agreement. If we had exclusive liberal-arts colleges that students were clamouring to get into, such places could impose a rigid curriculum on students, and some American colleges do this.

But in Canada, where the student as consumer of what universities have to offer is much more powerful, it's not likely that the old ways are going to return any time soon. Universities are smorgasbords for arts students: they can choose what they like, and they generally do. In this country—except for a certain level of literacy—there's currently nothing that all students should know.

6 Universities Don't Like Victory Lap Students

This may seem hard to believe, but it's true: a quarter of students who qualify to graduate from high school don't graduate. Instead they come back to school and take some of their courses over again—not because they have to, but because they want to. This costs them nothing and is a ridiculous waste of public funds that distorts the university admissions process.

The standard scenario is simple. Mary and John both get 78 per cent in Grade 12 Math. Both want to be accountants. Mary's parents encourage her to graduate. She does so and applies to her top three universities. She is turned down by all of them and either goes to a lower-ranked school or shifts into a less competitive program. John and his parents want into the top school. So he registers in Grade 12 again, takes a couple of courses, including Math 12, and gets his grade up to 85 per cent. He applies to university a year later, and armed with two or three higher grades, he is accepted.

Both students have the same abilities in math. But John, having spent thousands of dollars of public funds, gets a higher grade on the second pass (easy to do, since it's the same material) and so gets into the premium university program. Since most universities accept the higher of the grades, he has played the system well, even though he has the same potential as Mary.

It's not just the public system that offers the victory lap. There are many private high schools, some entirely credible and offering top-quality education, others little more than grade-selling education mills. Students sign up for the extra courses in these private institutes, secure the higher grade through some combination of hard work, excellent tutelage, or teacher complicity and apply to university with better scores.

This is a serious abuse, which universities could eliminate overnight by taking a few simple steps. First, they could announce that they will count only courses taken during the normal twelve years of study. Victory-lap courses would not be considered, except as evidence of students' determination to prepare themselves for advanced study.

Public schools should also eliminate the practice of providing free courses for victory-lap students. If John is a late bloomer or changes direction late in his high school career, exceptions could be made. Otherwise, the courses should be offered on a cost-recovery basis.

The third solution, which we have recommended in another chapter, would be the fairest: universities should establish their own entrance exams and simply ignore or seriously discount high school grades. These three actions—especially the third—would eliminate the academic incentives for redoing courses and remove the government subsidy for rule-bending grade building. Admissions would be more equitable—Mary would have the same chance of getting into accountancy school as John—and one of the silliest aspects of admissions gaming will have been eliminated.

7 Your Grades Will Drop

Here's some really bad news for incoming first-year students: you are likely to do worse—sometimes much worse—at university than you did in your last year of high school. It's called "grade shock," and a July 2010 study in *Maclean's* published some alarming statistics on it. On average, students drop ten points from, say, 82 per cent to 72 per cent, or A- to B-. Nearly a quarter drop by two grade points, for example from A- to C-. Another quarter do about the same as in high school. Only a tiny minority, 2.5 per cent, see their grades improve.

Many students who have been awarded entrance scholarships lose them at the end of the first year because of lower grades. Alarmingly, those who come to university with the highest marks suffer the biggest drop. It comes, of course, as a tremendous shock to a student who is unprepared for it. The student is horrified and dismayed, and the parents who saw their son or daughter off to university with a scholarship in hand are disappointed. It's bad news all round. Students become discouraged, and many drop out at the end of their first year. In some programs nearly half the students who begin a first year don't come back for a second. What a waste of time, money, and human potential.

There's no secret about the cause of grade shock. Students aren't any stupider than they were fifty years ago, though more of the less able ones come to university than before. They do spend less time studying at university, but not enough to explain the phenomenon. It's not even that high schools are failing to prepare them, though this is probably part of it. The answer is grade inflation.

When you read that incoming students at UBC now have high school grades that average 87 per cent—up from 80 per cent in 2000 and 70 per cent in 1990—you can see exactly what causes grade shock. There's also been some grade inflation at universities, but not as much. Inflated high school grades, fairly stable university grades. Thus the shock.

There was once a pretty good correlation between high school and university grades. Leaving aside students who came to university simply to party, a top-notch high school graduate usually did well at university. In fact, quite a number did better at university, because in those days, high school students usually had to take subjects they weren't good at (typically math and science). When they got to university and didn't have to take them, their grades improved. This doesn't happen anymore, because they don't have to take high school math beyond a fairly basic level.

The figure of 92 per cent we mentioned in Chapter 1 for students entering McGill is bound to lead to grade shock and is absurd on the face of it. What will happen when the figure reaches 100 per cent? How will they assess incoming students? On their bowling scores? Our universities and high schools are complicit in a shameful fraud in which the worst victims are the students themselves.

8 What to Look for in a Prof

You are heading for your first year at university. You are excited, but a little anxious. What are your profs going to be like? Kind? Weird? Boring? Fascinating? Nasty? All of the above? Fortunately, if you have a choice, you can preview them by asking older students, and by checking ratemyprofessors.com, the website where students rate their teachers. Here's what to look for—the qualities that make a great prof.

Caring. Caring doesn't mean touchy-feely, but a genuine desire to see students succeed, and a willingness to make an effort to bring this about. It's more than friendliness, and it's a quality that not all profs have. Will the prof help you get work experience? Does she care about you as a person? Not all do. Student comments about the highest-rated profs always include this quality.

Engaging. Does the prof present the material in an interesting way? There's almost nothing worse than a boring instructor. You really know what Einstein meant by relativity when you experience an hour-long class that seems to go on for a day. Lecturing or running a lab or a seminar is a skill not all profs have. Does she have irritating habits? Does he say "um" five times in each sentence, or "in this instance" forty times in an hour (students keep score—these twitches can drive them crazy.) Does he lecture with his back to the class?

Efficient. Is she well organized? Does he take forever to grade papers and hand them back? If profs aren't efficient, it may be because they care more about their careers than about you. Beware.

Respectful. Does he think that teaching first-year students is beneath his dignity? Surprisingly, some profs do. Does she answer your questions without rolling her eyes? We hope so.

Fair. You may think you want a prof without strong opinions, political and otherwise, but you don't—such a person is the mental equivalent of a cabbage. You want one who won't downgrade you for disagreeing with him—neither some right-winger who marks your papers down for being too politically progressive, nor a Marxist who does the opposite. There aren't many of these, but to be stuck in a class headed by one is deadly.

Knowledgeable. This goes without saying, and almost all profs are.

Famous. You may think it would be great to be in a class run by Professor X, the internationally renowned scholar. Unfortunately, these people are rare, and they don't often teach first-year courses. Unless you are heading for graduate school and want to be able to say that you studied with the famous Professor X this is a minor consideration.

We hope you find profs who have all these qualities. The good news is that universities take teaching much more seriously than they did a couple of generations ago. Most have "teaching and learning" centres that give courses on teaching techniques. Most let students rate profs anonymously at the end of the course, and sensible profs take the comments seriously. Things aren't perfect, but they are a great deal better than they used to be.

II
Planning a
University Career

9 Universities Want High Schools to Shape Up

Universities and high schools are in a quiet but undeclared war. Universities claim that the schools do not prepare students for first-year university. The high schools say that their role is to educate a diverse student population, not to be a minor league for universities.

It's not that high schools do a terrible job with their students. The problem is that a growing percentage of high school students are going on to university. Thirty years ago, when 15 per cent of high school graduates went to university, the quality of the students was pretty consistent. Now, with half the students doing so, the quality is more uneven.

High schools are right. They have a broader responsibility to prepare young people for adulthood. They cope with hostile students, interfering and often unsupportive parents, constant demands to adapt the curriculum, and growing responsibilities for moral and ethical training. They do this with little real power over the students and with a student-centred ethos that makes it increasingly difficult to manage classrooms and to ensure that students learn what they need to know. Imagine trying to run a high school in a province that insists that every child must graduate from high school, and at the same time keep standards at a level that will satisfy the universities. Unless you "stream" students, something that was abandoned a long time ago, the goals are incompatible.

Universities are right. Grade inflation has eaten away at the integrity of high school markets. When a majority of applicants have higher than 80 per cent averages, it's hard to take grades seriously. Students arrive at university with very uneven skills. High school graduation, even with high marks, does not mean the student can read for meaning, write in a grammatically correct fashion, handle advanced mathematics, or embrace complex scientific concepts.

Some students have all the needed skills and more, yet have lower high school grades than those who are less talented. The reason for this is that some very bright students find high school boring and they tune out, only to flourish when they get into university. Singling out such students is extremely difficult, however. Universities that admit students with grades in the 60s and 70s typically find very few such diamonds in the rough and encounter many more students who clearly are not up to the challenge of university.

What is to be done? Universities and high schools need to talk more. They need to identify the gap between Grade 12 and the first-year university requirements. Then they need to be clear about who is responsible for bridging the gap (in the United States this responsibility is falling mainly on the universities, largely because of the failings of the country's public education system).

Universities need to understand that high schools are not training programs. High schools must appreciate that many of the students they send to university will fail or drop out before graduation. Universities have to avoid the obvious solution, which is to lower standards and downgrade expectations in the first year.

But universities are not total patsies, and there is a secret they don't like to broadcast. Registrars, who are responsible for university admissions, know that not all high schools are the same. Over time, they collect data on the academic experience of graduates from individual schools. They can then handicap the students from outlier schools. If Nowhere Secondary School consistently gives overly generous grades, applicants from that school will have their grade averages discounted. An 80 per cent student from Nowhere

SS might get credit for a "real" standing of 76 per cent—and might miss out on admission. A student at a more highly rated school might submit a grade of 76 per cent but get credit for an 80 per cent average—and get admission. But this approach is a clunky workaround. There are much better solutions, one of which is a university admission exam.

Forget the BA: Now You Need Two Degrees

For decades, a Bachelor's degree was a ticket to the middle class. Until the 1970s, only about 10 per cent of high school graduates went on to complete a Bachelor's, which meant that fewer than 5 per cent of the population had one. We also had a very middle-management kind of country—with lots of jobs in the growing public service, the banks, the large retail operations, and the big industrial concerns that drove the Canadian economy.

Three big things have happened since then. First, the national economy has changed, and middle-management jobs have eroded steadily. Second, specialization became the foundation of corporate and government operations. There was less interest in generalists and more urgency in hiring people who could move directly into a line position. Where previously a degree in any science or arts discipline was a fine career-launching pad, increasingly companies now look for marketers, human resources professionals, or financial analysts.

Third, and most important of all, Canadian universities flooded the market. The once-rare undergraduate degree became ubiquitous. With close to 50 per cent of all high school graduates going on to post-secondary education, what had once been a mark of distinction and accomplishment now became a base qualification.

Between 1998 and 2008 the number of degrees, diplomas, and certificates awarded at university level increased by 48 per cent. The undergraduate degree became what the high school diploma was in the 1960s, a general indication of intellectual ability and motivation, and the starting point for career development. Ironically Canada has more need of people with trade skills than with basic undergraduate credentials, a fact brought into sharp relief when checking out job listings in major employment markets.

Companies and government agencies that once happily hired from the newly minted undergraduate degree holders have raised their expectations. Why not hire someone with a Master's degree? Universities (and government funders) recognized what was happening and began a very rapid expansion of graduate programs. Between 1999 and 2009, full-time undergraduate enrolment increased by 43 per cent, but graduate enrolment shot up by 70 per cent.

Students seeking a good career now understand that two degrees are generally required if they want to increase their chances of success. Some go back to community college to get a practical credential, but most aspire to white-collar careers. With a few exceptions, such as engineering, the second degree or a Master's degree has become commonplace. The number pursuing discipline-based graduate degrees (English, botany, and such) has not grown all that much, but there is an enormous demand for what are called professional Master's degrees and professional degrees.

The silver lining here is that the impending retirement of the baby boomers should create a very large number of openings for young people. If the projections hold, students in the next decade will face abundant employment opportunities, and Canadian companies and agencies will be scrambling to find qualified, hard-working, dependable people. Indeed, the country is already short of skilled workers in many crucial, largely technical fields and encourages immigration to fill the slots.

It seems unlikely, however, that the graduation patterns from Canadian universities will match the changing employment needs. Canada produces too many generalists—the basic undergraduate degree holders—and not enough specialists, particularly in technical areas. Rick Miner, former president of Seneca College in Ontario, produced a crucial report in 2010 on the future of employment in Ontario. The title captured the situation very nicely: *People Without Jobs, Jobs Without People*. According to Miner, the Canadian education system is producing many well-educated people, but not necessarily in the fields where the need is the greatest. For Ontario alone, there may be as many as 800,000 vacancies by 2016 and 2 million by 2031—at the same time unemployment rates will be growing dramatically.

Graduating students trying to make their way in an unfriendly and limited job market know and live the reality. The second degree has become a primary means of dealing with their career aspirations. It's clear, however, that universities and university students will have to continue to innovate and change if they are to keep up with the continually shifting economic situation.

A Degree Is Not Such a Hot Investment

For many years universities held out a carrot for advanced study—money. You will make much more money with a degree than if you stop your studies right after high school. How much money? The number—$1 million over the course of a career—was just the right size: impressive, but not ridiculous.

The math was simple: four years (or more) of study + an investment in tuition and accommodation = a much wealthier life. From every perspective, the numbers made sense and justified the expenditure.

But as a financial investment, a university education may look increasingly questionable. A study by Statistics Canada demonstrated that many university degrees provided a very small Return on Investment (ROI), lower than money placed in safe market investments. There were exceptions—engineering, accountancy, business, law, teaching, and medicine—but the general undergraduate degrees and non-professional Master's degrees in the humanities and some of the social sciences provided a small, in some cases negative, ROI. In Quebec, in 2001, the ROI for a history degree was about 5 per cent. Medicine was 20 per cent. A third of degree holders had a negative ROI. Ouch!

And the $1 million figure may no longer hold. A 2010 American study by *Bloomberg BusinessWeek* pegged the return from a degree from a public university at $330,000 over a lifetime—a decent sum, but worth all the time and effort? Canadian reports are revealing similar patterns.

There is a joke going around. "Universities," the line goes, "are where A students teach B students how to work for C students." With rich and famous college dropouts succeeding at the highest level—Bill Gates, Steve Jobs, Mike Lazaridis, and so on—there is a growing belief that university is, at best, a marginal investment. There is even a College Dropouts Hall of Fame that celebrates the accomplishments of those who never went to university or failed to complete their studies.

It's fashionable to knock the investment approach to post-secondary education and to highlight the reality that other factors—talent, creativity, motivation, work ethic, and just plain luck—may be just as important as having a university degree. But in general, the argument against university study is silly. Many university graduates succeed. And would you want doctors, lawyers, accountants, teachers, and other specialists to practice their professions without a degree? Entrepreneurs and creative people are in a different league, and the early stages of the tech revolution have created a large number of wealthy geeks who converted video-game playing and programming into billion-dollar fortunes. The success of the IT sector is not likely to carry over to highly specialized fields like nanotechnology and biotechnology.

Or look at it this way: do you have what Steve Jobs has—intelligence, drive, ruthless ambition? Are you willing to work a hundred hours a week and crush all opposition? Or are you a fairly normal person? If the answers to these questions are no, no, and yes, then perhaps you should consider a degree.

But also consider this. University costs a lot of money. If an undergraduate degree is a foundation for advanced study and a pathway into a profession, it is a good investment. If a student stops at an undergraduate degree or takes a more general arts or science degree, the financial return may be quite small. It is true, also, that some university degrees do not pay off: a recent study showed more than a third of college- and university-educated people aged twenty-five to twenty-nine in Canada were working at jobs for which they were overqualified. In dollar and cents terms, the students and their parents would do better to put their money in the bank and invest in different careers and lifestyle.

Universities, however, can offer a terrific investment in personal growth, citizenship, and all-round development. Financial accounting covers only a small portion of the value of a degree. There's more to life than money—honestly there is.

First University, then College

This may be hard to believe, but it's true. Twenty years ago, the British Columbia Institute of Technology revealed that its largest single source for students was the graduating class of the University of British Columbia. Students with Bachelor's degrees were going back to school—and at a college no less.

Such a thing was rare fifty years ago. Now, however, many university graduates go to college to transform their academic degree into a practical, employment-ready credential. Colleges are developing many one-year, post-degree programs specifically to meet this demand. They are much better than universities at connecting with employers—they are also more flexible in opening and closing programs, limiting and expanding enrolment, in line with realistic appraisals of job opportunities. For university students looking for work, college is a practical option.

Universities are uneasy about this trend. That fact that many university graduates "go back"—a weighted phrase—to college implies that universities have failed to prepare students for the job market. Governments resent paying twice for the same student: a full undergraduate degree and then a college diploma.

Colleges, though, like the arrangement. It provides them with a flow of well-educated, smart, and capable students who realize they need some practical training to get a job. Employers get employees who have both technical proficiencies of a college degree and the broad skill set and understanding of the university student.

There has long been an unspoken hierarchy in post-secondary education. Colleges do the practical, remedial, and hands-on stuff. Universities do the cerebral, professional, leading-edge things. But this distinction misses the quality, difficulty, relevance, and attractiveness of many of the newer college programs. Few university degree programs in Canada match Sheridan College's animation program for student career prospects and employer satisfaction. In many of the technical fields, colleges offer excellent, demanding, and career-ready programs that remain in very high demand.

The sad part in this educational pattern is that it reveals a lack of planning and foresight. Some students, if they had thought carefully about their options, might have gone directly to college—a perfectly fine choice that does not get the respect it deserves. Other students who "go back" to college often look on their university years as a waste of time, but later discover that combining college and university education is an excellent way to proceed. If Canada's post-secondary institutions operated as a system, there would be greater coordination of the growing list of educational options. Since that will not happen, students will continue on winding, uncertain, and sometimes unnecessary educational journeys.

Canadian Universities Are All Pretty Much the Same

Look at the program offerings for any six Canadian universities. You'll find they are all pretty much the same. It used to be that the big ones had graduate schools, while the smaller institutions concentrated on undergraduate degrees and teaching, but most of the small ones have added graduate programs and more research activity too. One department or one faculty is just like another.

There's a basic model for Canadian universities. Each is charged with being a local access point, responsible for bringing a broad menu of educational offerings to its region. Typically they add some teaching and research activity more specifically targeted to the local area: like UPEI's island studies, Dalhousie's oceanography program, Memorial's folk studies, Waterloo's co-operative education system, Saskatchewan's excellent First Nations programs, and Windsor's automotive engineering.

One of the strengths of America's university systems is its remarkable diversity. Its little-known institutions range from schools built around the great books to ones operating on Quaker principles. There are technology-rich schools and ones devoted to social justice. Most, but not all, are private. Places such as Evergreen College in Washington State have no counterpart in Canada. Religious institutions add character to the American system, ranging from the ultra-fundamentalist Bob Jones University to less extreme, inclusive colleges operated by more middle-of-the-road denominations.

In many other countries, particularly in East Asia, private universities with a sharp focus on career readiness are behind much of the diversity. These institutions are narrowly conceived—students interested in, say, information technology or dentistry can find a school designed specifically around their interests—and they don't try to be all things to all people, which is the Canadian approach.

As the Canadian and global economies continue to evolve rapidly, the country needs universities that respond more effectively to the diversity of interests among students and employers, that adopt different teaching styles, and that take unique approaches to campus life. There are some promising moves in this direction, particularly through such initiatives as the Great Northern Way campus (run by four institutions in Vancouver), OCAD University in Toronto, and a specialized multi-institutional nursing program in Prince Albert, Saskatchewan. But these are small steps, and all operate within the public sector. Private universities such as Quest and the on-line Meritus University hold potential, but remain only partially realized dreams.

The Canadian post-secondary system has risen, but without greater diversity it will fall—and the fall may be imminent. With wider choice and more variation it would better serve students and the country as a whole.

Universities Detest Helicopter Parents

She drove her daughter to the university and helped her move into residence. And then she wouldn't leave—her baby needed help adjusting to her first time away from home. So mummy stayed, sleeping on a mattress on the floor, for one week, then another, drawing complaints from students and irritating the residence managers. She left, reluctantly, after three weeks at least partially confident her daughter was in good hands.

She was an extreme example of a helicopter parent—people who hover over their university-age children—one of the strangest new aspects of university life. These are the same parents who produced the most cosseted children in history, coddled and pampered them from birth, and gave them all manner of material wealth and parental attention.

Now, two months after finally shepherding their children through high school, driving the teachers and administration half-crazy with their hovering, pestering, and general interference, they are being asked to stand down. The university wants to deal with the students—their legal clients—and not with parents. Shunted aside after years of providing a protective shell around their children, the parents don't know what to do. Universities are in a bind: they need parental money for tuition and residence fees. Other than that, though, the campus community wants the parents to keep their distance.

Helicopter parents, their hearts supposedly in the right place, like to interfere. Still thank heavens a small minority, they are quick to jump in if their kids fail a course, are accused of plagiarism, or otherwise run afoul of the university. They want to know their child is doing well. Some will call to check on class attendance and behaviour in residence. (We won't tell.) If Suzy fails a grade, the professor might well get a call and a demand for an explanation. In one well-remembered case, the mother admitted she had helped with research for a paper, assisted with writing, and proofread it carefully. She wanted a better grade for her work.

These parents can be tearful and soothing, or aggressive and demanding. They are known to accompany children to on-campus job interviews and to insist on an explanation if the job is not offered. (Hint to parents: showing up at the interview hurts the applicant. Stay away.)

These are the parents who walked their kids to school, would not let them go to the park until they were teenagers, and kept them under well-subsidized supervision until their late teens. The students, in turn, often lack an independence of spirit and turn readily to their parents for assistance long after the age when they should be independent.

Universities need to recognize the new parenting style and find ways to reach out to the helicopter moms and dads. Parents need to feel wanted, but they need to know that this hovering holds their children back and undermines the character-building aspects of the university experience. Universities could turn the situation to their advantage, as do American private schools, where these parents are seen not as pests but as potential major donors. Mommy and Daddy may find it hard to let go, but really, universities offer a great deal of support and encouragement.

Your baby has turned eighteen years old and is more than ready to leave the nest. Time to park the helicopter, turn off the engines, and sit back to enjoy the results of your nurturing.

It's About Careers, Not Education

A university education isn't what it used to be—and probably it never was! In an ideal world universities are about ideas, books, intellectual exchanges, and improving the world. In reality they are focused on training, career preparation, and various practical applications of theory—social work, education, or criminology. These are all good things, but they are often contradictory.

When universities talk about themselves, they speak of ideas, of the academy, of what they would call the "ivory tower" if that phrase had not gone out of fashion. They say that universities are for intellectual growth, for broadening minds, for "training people to think," for "life-long education," for equipping students with the intellectual skills to cope with a changing world. But what parents, governments, employers, and most students are looking for is preparation for a "meaningful" job, a well-paid one with regular hours where they get to tell people what to do and don't get their hands dirty. Applications for business programs flood in, and for career-focused degrees such as teaching, law, medicine, and information technology. Even the old disciplines of English and history have a large career-preparation aspect, for many students majoring in them plan to become schoolteachers.

In the 1970s, many young people came to university to learn about the world and to discuss "Big Ideas": the rights of women, homosexuals, and indigenous peoples, anti-colonialism, and early-stage environmentalism. Students hoped to change things for the better—and there were few enough of them that they could all find "meaningful" jobs.

The collapse of middle-class career opportunities in the 1980s and beyond altered the equation. People struggled to hold onto jobs through recessions and technological change. As the expansion of university education flooded the job market, suddenly a university education was no longer a virtual guarantee of career options.

Now it seemed that everyone had a degree, and there was talk that the MA was the new BA (see Chapter 10). One result was that even more young people came to university, since a degree was now the first filtering device for job applicants, as a high school diploma had been in the 1940s. As well, students became far more career oriented in their choice of program: if environmentalism was big, bring on a degree in environmental engineering; if the lumber industry was in the doldrums, forget the BSc in Forestry. Business schools flourished as never before.

But the universities remained largely locked in the 1960s and were unable to change quickly. While students began to flock to career-oriented disciplines, there was an oversupply of philosophy professors and too few in business.

The sad thing here is that a good liberal arts and science graduate is a great employee. Find a graduate who loves to learn, who reads well, thinks critically, and communicates effectively (not all of them, certainly), and you have a young adult who can go places. A philosophy or physics grad, properly equipped and motivated, is as valuable to employers and to society as any graduate of a practical or technical program. Brains are brains, and reasoning is reasoning—the skills are transferable. If we can figure out how to flag these great graduates, they can have it all: a terrific education and a start on a great career.

Your Success in Life Is Not Guaranteed by a University Education

A Canadian university was recognizing a highly successful graduate as engineering alumnus of the year. He loved the recognition but declared himself a bad choice. After all, he reported, he had done poorly in his courses and did not pass *summa cum laude* by any means. He got a job in the city as an engineer but lasted only a few weeks. The company liked him, but found his engineering skills deficient. He was transferred to marketing, where he flourished. Within a decade—and with the benefit of the dot.com boom—he was worth close to a billion dollars.

Was his success due to the university? Maybe, because he was better educated than he would have been otherwise. To his program? Perhaps, because engineering provides a first-rate approach to problem solving. But maybe he was just a smart, hardworking, and lucky guy. He might have done just as well without a university degree.

Universities love to point to their successful alumni as examples of the benefits of a university degree. But the causal connection is asserted, not proven. Think about it this way: Universities attract intelligent, motivated, hard-working, and often well-connected people. If they did not go to university they would still be just as intelligent, motivated, hard working, and connected.

Would they have been as successful in their careers without a degree? Not if they wanted to be architects, lawyers, or doctors. Universities are essential for those wishing to work in careers that require a solid foundation of knowledge and specialized skills. But a successful real-estate developer with two university degrees might have been just as successful without them.

How do you quantify the financial and career benefits of a university degree anyway? The hardest part is knowing if people's success is directly related to what they learned and studied at university. For those with entre-preneurial inclinations, the reality is probably mixed: the degrees help a little bit, but energy, motivation, and risk-taking matter more. The truth is that universities are not the seedbeds for such people or for anyone else seeking a career where the same qualities are the underpinnings of success.

Universities are being encouraged to teach and train entrepreneurs. If the observation above is correct—that universities do well with people looking for knowledge and skills-rich careers and much less well with the risk-taking, free-wheeling entrepreneurs—then expectations about success in this area need to be kept in check. A different kind of institution, one that likely does not exist (although the University of Waterloo and the University of Sherbrooke are moving in this direction), may be required if the goal is to create an entrepreneurial class in Canada.

University Fees Discriminate Against the Poor

What percentage of the costs of running a university do you think have anything to do with the undergraduate experience? There's quite a list of things that don't: graduate teaching, faculty sabbaticals, faculty research time (the argument goes that faculty research improves the undergraduate experience, but this is unproven), research laboratories and offices, library holdings that mainly benefit graduate students and faculty members, expensive scientific equipment and the support staff needed to run them, as well as university research, fundraising, alumni, recruiting, and com-mercialization offices.

None of these has much to do with undergraduates, yet they pay 50 per cent of the costs of operating the entire university—they may pay 80 per cent or more of the cost of the teaching and other services that are targeted directly at them. And low-income students are more likely to be under-graduate than graduate students.

No less a left-wing icon than Bob Rae has accurately described low tuition fees as one of the largest tax transfers to the upper-middle class in the country. It's not just a matter of saving students, or the taxpayers, money. There are broad socio-political issues connected with the question. Canadian university students come disproportionately from the ranks of the upper- and upper-middle classes. Children of the poor and lower-middle class are significantly less likely to attend university. Even with the availability of student loans, bursaries, university scholarships, and the like, poor families are much less likely to send their children to university.

It follows that the incentives for post-secondary education go dispro-portionately to the rich. They can shelter money in Registered Educational Savings Plans, which provide tax-free interest savings when applied to education. The Government of Canada supplements those contributions with a payment of 20 per cent (up to $400 a year) to encourage more sav-ing. Guess which economic group is more likely to put money aside for its children's university education, the single parent earning $30,000 a year or the two-income family pulling in $150,000?

Because fees are deductible, a wealthy family will pay some $2,600 a year less for its child to attend university than will a poorer family. This is why Bob Rae expressed such dismay at the NDP's continued insistence on lower university tuition fees, which remain a major subsidy for the wealthiest people in the country.

Canada's supposedly fair approach denies universities the tuition money that they need—and that many students can afford to pay—while not ensuring that students from poorer families can actually afford to attend university. We offer the promise of inclusiveness, but provide inequality of opportunity. Canada's best option would be to allow tuition fees to increase dramatically but to require universities and/or government bursary and loan schemes and grants to help students from lower-income backgrounds. A $10,000 tuition fee is as affordable for wealthy families as a $2,000 a year charge is for poor families.

Instead of tinkering with existing student loan arrangements—which can be very complex and often don't help those in greatest need—a program of financial assistance for students from low-income families is required. Without a real change like this, coupled with a major outreach initiative to reach the parents and school counsellors of these young people, the Canadian university system will become even more guilty of abetting income inequality in Canada.

Changing the system so that students from poor families actually have a greater chance of attending university would also address one of the greatest inconsistencies and shortcomings of the Canadian university system—namely that they have increasingly become subsidized job-training institutions for our wealthier fellow citizens. But this is unlikely to happen: the middle classes won't like it at all, and they are the ones who vote.

III
Inside the Ivory Tower

Not Every University Is "World Class"

"Excellence" is a word universities use a lot. The students are excellent, the faculty is excellent, and the facilities are excellent (except when they need more money, in which case they are substandard). Overall, they are "world-class," which is even better than excellent. But are they all equally excellent? Of course not, but you would never know it from promotional materials and presidential speeches.

Maclean's annual ratings—hated by all universities except the ones that top the list—tell us that this is not so. Employers know it's not so, as do the students who are aware enough to care. And faculty members know there's a pecking order.

Canada prizes and demands equality of access and treatment—in universities as much as in health care. But all Canadians know that, for first-rate care their children are better off at Sick Kids in Toronto than at the hospital in The Pas, Manitoba. So it is with universities.

The gap between the top Canadian institutions and the rest is growing. Not so long ago, working conditions, wages, and research opportunities (but not libraries and laboratories) were fairly equal across the country. No longer. Programs such as the Canada Research Chairs have shovelled

51

huge resources into the high-ranked places—the so-called "medical-doctoral institutions." These places also benefit the most from fundraising campaigns. The myth that all Canadian universities are equally excellent persists, but the reality is very different.

Canadian universities have not admitted publicly that there is a large diversity of experience and performance in our institutions. A 2010 report on universities declared, "all Ontario universities are research intensive." This is nonsense. The University of Toronto is research intensive. Algoma University is not.

American schools figured this out long ago. In the United States, there's a wide diversity among colleges and universities. Junior colleges focus on teaching lower-income kids at academic risk, and they don't expect their faculty to do much, if any, research. Expensive liberal arts colleges emphasize high-quality instruction and a rich student experience. Medical-doctoral institutions are research powerhouses.

The United States has many rating systems. If your alma mater is not a top-ranked research school or academically strong, it might be a top party place or have the best sports teams. No one thinks that the (fictional) University of Southern North Dakota is the same as Yale. But Americans do understand—much better than Canadians—that any one of a hundred small colleges may be a better place for some students than the Ivy League and research-intensive schools.

But not in egalitarian Canada. Here, everyone is excellent at, it seems, everything. Save for *Maclean's* and an effort by the *Globe and Mail* to rank the student experience, we seem to disavow hierarchies of achievement and quality, even if we know in our hearts they are there.

The plain fact is that not all places are excellent, nor (by definition) can they all be above average. The academic ability of the students at Waterloo is better than those at the University of Winnipeg. Researchers at Dalhousie outperform their provincial counterparts at Cape Breton University. The quality of the student experience at Acadia is much superior to that of York, and Mount Alison develops much stronger loyalty than mega-versities like the University of Alberta. That's just the way it is, and it's not necessarily a bad thing.

Great things are happening at all institutions. Weaker students can get strong assistance at open-access institutions like Brandon and the

University of New Brunswick, Saint John. Regina is no McGill, but in select areas (police studies, Great Plains research) it is the best in Canada. The sense of community is much better at the University of Saskatchewan than at the University of British Columbia. The law school at the University of Victoria isn't as well known as the University of Toronto's, but in fields like Aboriginal law it is outstanding. Aboriginal students are well supported at the University of Northern British Columbia; Vancouver Island University and Thompson Rivers University serve international students superbly.

Canada needs to drop the preoccupation with similarity and abandon the language of uniform excellence. Universities must focus on the specific qualities and abilities of their students, the problems and opportunities of their host region, and the limits of their resources. They need to celebrate their specific identities and strengths, not parrot fairy tales about the uniform excellence and similarity of the Canadian post-secondary system.

Our Universities Need a Proper Admissions Test

Canadian universities educate and train undergraduates. Their raw material is high school students. Universities know how to select the students by themselves and could easily do so if they wanted to. But they don't, and won't.

Instead universities let high schools and high school teachers perform this critical function. But why? Why do they outsource the single most important decision in their operations? Universities in general have strong reservations about the value of high school grades (see Chapter 9), even though they won't say so in public. Despite this, high school grades are the main criterion used by universities to evaluate applications.

There are other ways of doing things. Many American universities combine results from Standardized Aptitude Tests (SAT) with high school grades, or GPAs (grade point averages, as the universities call them). Some require essays as well. Others ask for lengthy personality profiles and face-to-face interviews. The top Japanese schools have their own entrance exams, for which applicants have to pay up to $1,000 for the privilege of writing. At places like Yale or Duke it often helps to have a parent who went there too, and then gave the place millions! That makes you a "legacy student," and you go to the head of the line. We don't recommend this—buying your way into university seems just too un-Canadian.

Our schools, in contrast, rely on a single set of numbers, produced by people over whom the universities have no control. By adopting this method of doing things Canadian universities have chosen to play a minimal role in the selection of their own students. It's amazing that universities have so little control over the calibre of incoming students. Imagine any other business turning over its quality control to a separate agency with a demonstrably uneven track record.

The solution is simple. Universities can establish their own admission tests. They can do this individually or collectively. The tests can be faculty- or program-specific, generic, scholarly, personality-based, or some combination of these. Students can be charged for writing the exam (to cover marking and administration costs). A private SAT-type service could be provided, or the universities could do all the testing themselves, according to their own requirements and standards. Open-entry institutions wouldn't need such an admission test, although its absence would draw attention to their lower standards.

Universities need basic information about applicants. Can they read at an advanced level? Can they write effectively? Do they have the necessary reasoning, numeracy, and analytical skills? Are they keen on learning what the university has to teach? Specialized programs, such as engineering and architecture, will have special questions to ask. The results of these tests, reviewed and analyzed over time, will provide valuable input into the admissions process.

This is not a new concept, even for Canada. Most law schools in the country require students to write the Law School Admission Test (LSAT). Architecture schools and some accounting programs have entrance tests.

Medical schools, of course, put applicants through a rigorous and intense exam and interview process.

A handful of elite universities—three or four to start—should break out from the pack. They claim they want the best scholars. They should prove it. If the top institutions implemented a test, the best students would still apply. A high school graduate is not going to switch from Toronto to Laurentian just because there is a three-hour test to write to get into the U of T.

Universities need to reclaim full responsibility for their admission decisions. They should pick students with a high chance of succeeding. Admission tests will do this. At the very least, they will give universities less reason to whine about the dismal standards of high schools.

Why will there be no admission test any time soon in Canada, outside the professional programs? One reason is that, unlike the situation in the United States, even the best Canadian universities don't have huge numbers of applicants. Unlike the elite American places, they don't turn down 90 per cent of their applicants, and they don't want to discourage any student from applying.

It's significant too that these admission tests come from the United States—and "American-style" is one of the worst things you can say about an idea in much of Canada. Why not let everyone have a chance at the University of Toronto? That's the Canadian way. Too bad. Universities will continue to outsource admission decisions, much to the detriment of many students and the universities themselves.

20 Our Math Students Just Can't Compete

A few years back, the *Japan Times* ran a story about the status of math education in that country that included a copy of a math exam. Math teachers in the United States remarked that the test looked like a first-year university final math exam. In fact, the test was from the compulsory national examination—not a tough one given to science students, but a much easier one given to high school students planning to study humanities at university. Humanities!

We live in a scientific age, where a high level of mathematical literacy is essential for national competitiveness in the fast-moving new economy. Stock markets work at hyper speed, driven by complex algorithms. The digital media sector requires thousands of workers with mathematical abilities. Engineers and applied scientists are needed in huge numbers to capitalize on the commercial possibilities of clean technology, biotechnology, nanotechnology, and many other science-based -ologies. Numeracy and mathematical ability are essential in business—particularly in accounting. They play a critical role in medicine and health care, and are increasingly important in the social sciences. Math has emerged as a core requirement for jobs in our modern economy.

Canadian thirteen-year-olds are ranked eighteenth in the world in both math and science by the Trends in International Math and Science Study. In a different study, we ranked tenth in math skills in 2009, down from seventh three years earlier. Results are not even across the country. Alberta tops the Canadian rankings, and urban schools do better than rural ones.

But the major issue for Canada is that not enough students are going into math-based undergraduate and graduate degrees. An astonishingly high percentage of Math PhD candidates at North American universities are international students. Would you have guessed more than 90 per cent? There is an ethnic twist to this issue as well. Students of Asian ancestry, particularly new Canadians, dominate the enrolment in Canadian universities in math.

Canadian faculties of math, computer science, and engineering work very hard to attract more Canadian students. The University of Waterloo's Faculty of Mathematics—the largest in the world—operates an international test of mathematical proficiency and received a multi-million dollar grant from the Gates Foundation to expand the global reach of the examination. Other schools try just as hard and make substantial—and only marginally successful—efforts to attract more female students. But the main point is that there are not enough Canadian math students at Canadian universities.

Explanations abound: poor teaching in elementary and high school, poor instruction at university, a subject matter that many students find unappealing, an absence of role models for young math scholars, a male/geek culture that repels women, and a weak understanding of career opportunities in the field. The lack of student interest is not new, which means parents are not always helpful or academically supportive. Perhaps there is a simpler explanation: math is hard and requires a lot of work. Class work must be supplemented by hours of practice and repetition.

Canada needs to make major advances in math education and to engage students in math. The country needs a significant improvement in the emphasis given to mathematics and related fields in high schools. Improving the training and professional development of math teachers would help. Universities should require Grade 12 math for applicants to all programs and program-specific math courses should be required across the university.

More importantly, the country needs a fresh approach to math education. Numeracy is as important as literacy in the twenty-first century. National competitiveness requires Canadian students to be prepared for the realities of the modern workforce. Without a substantial increase in the number of math-savvy graduates, Canada will have difficulty attracting and holding new-economy and tech-based companies in the country.

21 Killing the Traditional Disciplines

What do we mean by traditional disciplines? We mean those disciplines that date from the nineteenth century, when universities escaped the control of the churches and began to teach literature, history, and the social, natural, and physical sciences. These are, or were, the core disciplines at Canadian universities.

Up to 1960 this core was unchallenged, with the addition of new social sciences (for example sociology, psychology), new professional disciplines (nursing, education, architecture), and new physical sciences deriving from new discoveries (nuclear physics). The vast majority of students studied in the central academic fields. Emerging interdisciplinary programs in the 1960s and 1970s—Canadian studies, Native studies, women's studies, labour studies, and the like—had a relatively small impact.

In the past twenty years, students have been voting with their feet for disciplines that promise lucrative careers. New fields like business and commerce have grown rapidly—more business degrees are granted each year in North America than Bachelor of Arts degrees. The traditional disciplines reacted by creating new interdisciplinary programs, like international studies, law (as an undergraduate degree, a huge success at Carleton University), criminology or legal studies, administrative studies (one of the largest majors at the University of Western Ontario), and degrees oriented towards the helping professions and pre-professional programs.

Canada has so far avoided excesses such as the Bachelor of Surf Science at Edith Cowan University in Australia, but new program development has continued apace. The percentage of students majoring in traditional disciplines—particularly in the languages and literature programs—continues to drop, in some cases sharply. As a result, academics in these fields seek new ways of packaging and presenting their material in the hope of attracting student attention. Some of these new initiatives draw on contributions from the traditional disciplines and are demanding, intellectually exciting, and very career focused, including programs in nanotechnology, digital media, gerontology, and various branches of environmental studies. Critics see others as academically weak, lacking in rigour, and overly focused on faddish student interests—studying comic books or the Harry Potter novels in English departments, for example.

External support matters too. Business schools have been bolstered by substantial amounts of government funding, employer demand, and donor support. Only one arts faculty—the Irving K. Barber School of Arts and Sciences at UBC Okanagan—has attracted similar support.

The shift in student and public interest, and the loss of centrality for the traditional disciplines, presents universities with a huge challenge. The old disciplines have been around for a long time by Canadian standards, and the fences that separate and protect them are high. Most administrative and faculty resources are based in the standard disciplines, even if the students are flocking to new fields. Professors from the older disciplines still dominate the decision-making committees, making it tough to reallocate resources to growing programs.

With students (and often government funding and employer interest) focused in one direction, and with university resources and priorities focused in different ones, universities are caught in a dilemma. Change is difficult and in a way undesirable, for traditional scholarly values and approaches are a strength of the university system. Universities are being torn in two directions, with powerful forces of tradition (disciplines, academic departments, and established programs) aligned in opposition to equally powerful forces for change (employers, students, and interdisciplinary scholars seeking to break away from the standard fields). There's no easy solution to this problem.

The Power of Business Schools

Thirty years ago, business schools in Canada were fairly humble places. Many of the faculty had only Master's degrees, and they published less, and differently, than most of their academic colleagues.

What a difference a generation or two can make. Business schools are now the BMOC (Big Man on Campus, a sexist phrase from the 1950s). They attract large numbers of applicants, including many of the best students. Accountancy programs have the same prestige as engineering, medicine, and law. Business leaders across the country pay handsomely to have their names associated with these schools: Rogers (at Ryerson), Sauder (UBC), Haskayne (Calgary), Schulich (York), Sobeys (Saint Mary's), and others, including perhaps the most prestigious, Ivey, at the University of Western Ontario—all of them named after their major donors. As well, high-cost MBA programs and even higher-tuition executive MBA programs provide a steady infusion of funds.

One result of this Niagara of money is sky-high salaries. A beginning accounting prof can make twice as much as a beginning English one. Senior business faculty members can make as much as some university presidents. Many faculty also make even more money by consulting part time.

What's at work here is the academic application of market forces. The schools seem unstoppable, and universities that do not play along will probably lose faculty and students. Recently, Canada had nearly twenty times as many job openings for academic jobs in accounting as there were new PhDs in that discipline. Compare that with history—the University of Toronto alone produces more PhDs than there are tenurable posts available in the entire country. And students pay for, and fight to get into, business programs because the return on their investment is higher than for most other degree programs.

But the success of business programs distorts campus environments the same way that medicine did forty years ago. Other faculty naturally would like the salaries that business profs make, even though the dynamics of the job market are markedly different. Many cast envious eyes on the business school facilities—attractive buildings, high-end technology—and professional environment.

Reaction to the success of business programs emerges in different forms: anger at the reallocation of university resources, suggestions that business as a discipline is academic rubbish, and claims that the business donors are manipulating and distorting campus life.

The story is far from being all negative. Specialized programs, such as the University of Saskatchewan's Aboriginal business offerings, and early-stage e-commerce studies at the University of New Brunswick, have had a clear and positive effect. Roger Martin of the Rothman School of Management at the University of Toronto and Jack Minz of the University of Calgary are but two examples of prominent business academics who have had a real impact on the Canadian business environment. The overall career impact of Canadian business education may be over-stated—the country produces many more managers than entrepreneurs and there may now be a glut of MBA programs on the market—but the schools are generally making a difference.

Business school leaders and business executives have long pushed for an expansion of enrolment and research. The cynic in us feels compelled to point out that a quarter-century of rapid growth in business schools has been matched by a comparable period of decline in Canadian productivity and competitiveness. We hasten to add, however, that business schools are not the cause of Canadian commercial problems—but it's also not clear if they are the answer.

Business schools have led several of the most significant trends in contemporary academic affairs: the push for more professional education, donor-driven expansion, responsiveness to student and employer demands, highly integrated business-campus relations, high tuition fees for market-based programs, greater autonomy for professional schools, unequal distribution of resources on campuses, the marginalization of traditional disciplines, the rise of new commercially based research and teaching, and increased student emphasis on career opportunities. Business schools did not cause or create these trends, but they have certainly capitalized on them. It is, of course, in their nature to do so.

A Nasty Secret

There's a nasty secret that rarely surfaces in public discussions about universities. Many students—at some places perhaps nearly half of all of those who enter—do not graduate. Across the country, tens of thousands of students each year leave campuses, some to transfer to other educational institutions, others for jobs. But the vast majority leave as academic failures.

Think about that for a moment. Remember how much time and effort young Johnny devoted to picking a university, paying tuition and room and board, and launching his studies? Now, imagine how he feels when he fails three or four mid-term exams, struggles with essays and lab reports, crashes during final tests, and then gets the dreaded Dean's letter requiring an extended academic holiday, often in mid-year when his probation runs out. Contemplate the phone call: "Hi, Mom. I got kicked out of school. Can. I come home?"

So much is loaded into this experience. Forget the money; you can write that off as an unfortunate investment. Remember that young people, coddled from birth, have little experience with failure. They have been told that prosperity and opportunity require a university degree. They know their future depends on it. And now they have been rejected by the institution that was the repository of their career ambitions. Failure in university is a life-limiting experience.

Why is the failure rate so high? Even the best schools, attracting only the top students, lose up to 10 per cent of their first-year students. Issues of maturity, too much beer, the discovery of sex, wrong program choices, laziness, homesickness, and money woes are part of the challenge.

But the real culprit is the national conceit that all students who want to go to university should have the chance. University, according to this belief, is a right, like shelter and medical care. Other countries limit access to (publicly funded) universities to students who have demonstrated aptitude and motivation.

No such elitism for Canada. Even the top schools are comparatively accessible. Our national mantra about equality of opportunity is no better displayed than through the expensive university admission processes. Universities need money to survive. Students provide money. Therefore students are heartily welcomed, with inadequate concern about their ability to succeed.

The current approach is wrong. Students who fail carry a heavy personal burden. Their parents are disappointed—with their child or the institution—as well as out of pocket. The cost to government is considerable. And classes with large numbers of students ill suited for study can produce a very unhappy academic environment.

There is enormous variation in academic success rates. Universities that attract more students of lower academic achievement (below 75 per cent is a good cut-off, given today's grossly inflated high school grades) have lower graduation rates. The data on this crucial topic is collected but is rarely disseminated and does not form part of the *Maclean's* ranking of universities—even though it may be the single most important measure of institutional effectiveness.

Greater honesty is needed here. A dismally large portion of the students going to a Canadian university in any academic year will not graduate. If incoming students knew this secret, some of the weaker ones might find a better training option elsewhere. Others might be more motivated and might work harder, knowing how many actually do fail and are asked to leave. This dirty little secret needs to be aired.

There's a Good Reason So Many University Buildings Are Ugly

And the answer is they're cheap. Beauty, elegance, grace, and tradition cost a lot more than big-box functionality. The people who build universities—governments—are usually unwilling to pay the extra cost for beauty.

The traditional style for universities was "collegiate Gothic," a phrase that suggests something medieval. Gothic style—stone construction (usually now just for facing over steel beams), pointed windows, and the suggestion of towers and other castle- or church-like details—has had a powerful influence on university architecture. It can be found all over North America on college campuses, especially those built before 1960. Think Duke, Boston College, and Princeton in the United States; or Queen's, Toronto, Western Ontario, and Saskatchewan, in Canada. And many others in both countries.

Since about 1970, new construction in the collegiate Gothic style has become quite rare. Cost didn't matter before 1960, when labour was cheap. It didn't matter to the provincial governments that wanted lasting memorials to their wisdom in patronizing education, or to rich benefactors like the Massey family, who built Hart Hall at the University of Toronto. It did, however, matter to governments in the 1960s, when universities were springing up like toadstools. Preformed concrete replaced stone. And collegiate Gothic buildings were hardly sexy. No architect was going to become famous putting up these old-style buildings, so when the 1960s came along, there was a market for new architectural ideas in universities.

In Canada the most famous of these ideas came from the brain of Arthur Erickson, who is responsible for Simon Fraser University, a great dark, damp, ominous pile of concrete on the top of Burnaby Mountain in Vancouver, and for the University of Lethbridge. Lethbridge, though, has been much improved by recent additions, and now manages to take even better advantage of its unique setting. Simon Fraser has been much praised, but to us it is suggestive of the Ministry of Love in Orwell's *1984*. Being on the campus makes us want to scream, "No, not Room 101! Anything but Room 101."

Poured concrete gave us many seriously ugly campus buildings all over Canada. Every province has examples. Look at Lakehead University in Thunder Bay—not the lovely setting but the strikingly cheap-looking buildings. Look at the University of Regina (except for the new Fine Arts area), or McMaster's hideous teaching hospital that obliterated part of the Royal Hamilton Botanical Gardens. Look at Concordia in Montreal, or the University of Winnipeg (though these have the excuse of being downtown campuses) or the Université de Moncton, which looks like a light industrial park. Better still, don't look.

Not that all contemporary campus architecture is bad. Where local influences have prevailed, some lovely buildings have gone up: the Whitehorse campus of Yukon College, the interior built of peeled logs, is one example, and there are others, including UNBC, the wonderful Barber Centre at UBC, and the stunning K.C. Irving Environmental Centre at Acadia.

The campus of Ryerson University in Toronto is a good demonstration of the contrast between old and new. The campus is built in a totally undistinguished style—odd for a place that gives a degree in architectural science. In the middle of a grassy quadrangle, however, part of the façade of a building that once stood on the site has been preserved: the original teachers' college for Ontario. It was built 150 years ago in the Greek Revival style, with large imposing windows and door, square columns, and a frieze running around the top. It fairly shouts "serious thinking stuff going on here," while the rest of the campus looks like a series of hives for bureaucrats. (But Ryerson does get full credit for reviving Maple Leaf Gardens as part of the campus.)

What the people who commissioned the designs for these older buildings—Grant Hall at Queen's, University College at Toronto, the original buildings at UBC, Saskatoon, Western, and McMaster—had in mind for their campuses, whether they were Gothic, Romanesque, or classical, was that they have *gravitas*—Latin for "stature, authority, dignity, formality in bearing and appearance." Alas, gravitas has been replaced by functionality, accessibility, and inclusiveness. These are not bad things either, but when the old style went, higher education lost some of its soul.

25 We Aren't Producing Engaged Citizens

Universities were going to change the world. It was the 1960s and social ferment was everywhere. Women were under-represented. Bring them in—and in they came. Minorities had too small a place on campus. Open the doors—and in they came. Subtle and not so subtle restrictions limited opportunities for Jews, Aboriginal people, and others. Change the rules, be accessible—and changes were made. Ensure people of working-class backgrounds could afford to go to university, and that they knew of the opportunities. Money was found—and openings created. Satellite campuses were built in smaller communities to increase accessibility. Done and done again.

The promoters of the university system got all they asked for and more, but did education transform the nation and the world? Participation rates soared, accessibility expanded, new groups of students attended, and radical academic perspectives replaced stodgy orthodoxy. On the social front, universities have been at the forefront of many key revolutions—gay rights, women's rights, Aboriginal rights—and have established traditions of acceptance and tolerance that, though hard won, have been replicated outside the campuses. Racism has moderated, or at least gone underground. More students have access to the economic opportunities attainable through advanced education, although these seem to be backsliding of late. Graduates seem to have been well trained for jobs. There is much on the positive side of the ledger.

But the good news seems to have faded. Participation rates in politics, particularly through elections, are woefully bad and getting worse. Civic responsibility, as seen through charitable donations and volunteerism, is far from impressive (a quarter of the population does most of the giving). Interest in international affairs remains amazingly marginal—particularly surprising given the multicultural nature of the population. The country's devotion to innovation—and, indeed, the country's commitment to the concept of Canada—seems fragmented at best. When was the last time Canadians got truly excited about a new national initiative? Ask Stéphane Dion what the country thought of the "Green Shift."

Contrast the 2010s with the 1970s. Forty years ago, universities in Quebec led the political turmoil of Quebec separatism. Western Canadian universities were at the forefront of the western alienation debate (the University of Calgary has maintained a reputation in this regard, but the other western schools have gone quiet). Maritime institutions pushed for recognition of the unique situation in that region. There were great debates, strongly influenced by university academics, about national social programs, regional economic development, social policy, and the like. These were passionate and even exciting times for a country that seems to recoil at both passion and excitement.

There are few such debates these days. Perhaps in the 1970s they were simply reflecting the *zeitgeist*. The energy and ideas may have come as much from the public as from the institutions. It is interesting that the continued growth of the university system has not resulted in a burst of citizenship and engagement, has not produced a flood of ideas on how to improve and develop Canada. Instead, the universities have become solid contributors to the economic development of the country, rather than focal points for debates about Canada's future. Perhaps—and this is being nostalgic and wistful—Canadians expected more from the expansion of our universities. It says a lot about the changing nature of our country that a growth spurt launched out of enthusiasm for change has resulted in a system that is comfortable maintaining the status quo.

26 Medical Students Are Getting a Free Ride

Every year, medical doctors educated in Canada leave for the United States. The number spiked in the mid-1990s, when about five hundred left, though it's less than that now. Some do come back though, and in 2006, about sixty more returned than left. Over time, however, more than 10 per cent of doctors trained here have ended up in the United States.

Whatever the number, the fact that it costs close to half-a-million dollars to train a doctor, most of which is paid by the taxpayer, amounts to a considerable financial loss to Canada, to say nothing of the fact that our aging population needs all the doctors we can get.

What's the solution? We could waive tuition for doctors who agree to practice in Canada, especially in small or remote communities, for a number of years after graduation. This is the principle on which the military colleges operate—their students must serve a period in the armed forces as the price of their education. Or we could make medical students sign a contract promising to pay the entire cost of their education if they leave the country within a certain period after graduation. Governments are already trying to persuade doctors to practice in rural areas—Liberal leader Michael Ignatieff announced a proposal along these lines in the summer of 2010.

None of this is likely to happen though, mostly because there's a huge element of hypocrisy involved in complaining about the situation. We are guilty too, for we do to the Philippines, South Africa, and other countries the same thing that the United States does to us—we poach their doctors. If it hadn't been for doctors fleeing South Africa in the 1990s, large sections of Saskatchewan, for example, would have been virtually doctorless. In 2006, 22 per cent of doctors practising in Canada were trained in foreign countries, most of which are poorer than we are. So we can't really complain: what's sauce for the goose...

27 Toronto Rules the Canadian Academic World

Canadians love to hate Toronto. They cheer when the Maple Leafs flounder—as they always do. They find secret pleasure when snowstorms bring "Hogtown" to a halt and find *schadenfreude* in the unending traffic jams on Highway 401. But in the university world, the power of the Greater Toronto Area and, particularly, the larger metropolitan area cannot be ignored.

The concentration of academic power in the GTA (and nearby in southern Ontario) is something to behold. The University of Toronto, Canada's largest (70,000 students at all campuses), and one of the best public universities in the world, dominates the system. The president of U of T has great access to federal and provincial governments, donors, and decision-makers. Its two satellite campuses—Scarborough and Mississauga—are growing quickly. Other institutions are only an hour or two away (or would be if all the other cars would get off the road).

York University, often controversial and with 50,000 students, Canada's second-largest English university (the Université de Montréal has 55,000), also has a French language campus in the city. Within a three-hour drive lie Guelph, McMaster, Brock, Waterloo, Wilfrid Laurier, Western Ontario,

Trent, and Queen's. Three of Canada's newest universities—Ryerson, Ontario College of Arts and Design University, and University of Ontario Institute of Technology—are in the GTA.

Two things stand out. First, the institutions listed above have close to 300,000 students—between a quarter and a third of all Canadian university students. No other part of Canada can match the scale, quality, and impact of the GTA institutions. Montreal comes the closest and has one of the highest student per 1000 people ratios in North America, but the collective impact tracks well behind Toronto. To the extent that universities drive national prosperity, Toronto has a huge advantage over all other areas.

Second, and more ominous, the GTA is far and away the largest source of future students in Canada. The metro region believes that it is short some 75,000 spaces—more than all the university students in Nova Scotia—and there is enormous pressure to open new campuses or brand new institutions.

For the foreseeable future Toronto will continue to dominate the Canadian university landscape. Indeed, the concentration of academic power in the GTA is probably greater than the city's corporate authority, which has been sliding slowly towards the West. Academically—hard as it is for some of us to accept—Toronto is the centre of the Canadian academic universe. Hogtown rules.

28 Sports Rule...Or Not

We (the authors) agree on many subjects, but there are two on which we cannot see eye to eye. The first is the place of athletics at Canadian universities. Our differences seem irreconcilable, so we offer both positions, and invite readers to make their own choices.

On the one hand...

One of the several ways that United States universities march to the sound of a different drummer is the matter of intervarsity athletics. The multi-billion dollar, television-enriched, hyper-competitive extravaganza that is American college sports has no counterpart anywhere else in the world.

Intervarsity sports in Canada are not like this. A few basketball teams pack in the fans. A game at Bishop's or St. Francis Xavier is a wonderful community experience. Sitting on metal stands at a Saskatoon Huskies football game is to understand why Saskatchewan is such a great place and what Prairie pride is all about. But compare this to the 80,000 fans jammed into a U.S. college football game or the thousands of "Cameron Crazies" (Duke university sports fanatics) camped out for days to grab a ticket to the Duke versus North Carolina basketball game, and you will realize that Canada plays minor league.

The vast majority of Canadian intervarsity athletics—and the athletes and coaches—represent the ideal of classical sport: participation for the love of it and the chance to push oneself to excel. Many players have to cover some of their own expenses for competing and live with poor facilities, part-time coaches and very little attention. Coaches accept pitiful stipends and put in hundreds of hours to support their athletes. Crowds rarely extend beyond family members and girl/boyfriends, and the events are mostly ignored by the press. There is honour, blood, sweat, and tears, but little glory in the life of the Canadian student athlete.

University can and should build their campus life around recreational and intervarsity athletics. Cheering for the campus team against cross-province rivals is great fun. The student athletes—provided they are both students as well as athletes—are superb ambassadors and great community builders. The melding of body, mind, and spirit has been a goal of humanity for centuries—check out the bios of Canada's astronauts if you have any doubts—and should be a central feature of campus life. Canadian campuses have too little in the way of athletics and too little sport as part of campus life. Game time!

On the other hand…

You can also argue that athletics have the potential to seriously corrupt universities.

It really depends on what kind of athletics you are talking about. There can be no quarrel with the idea that participation in sports for the sake of sport can be character building. No one objects to a university sponsoring a volleyball, fencing, track, swimming, or other team, or to the major sports—football, basketball, hockey—played intramurally.

The problem arises with the major intervarsity sports—that is, the major sports played between universities. These are the ones that people want to watch, and they are the expensive ones. With this importance comes the possibility of corruption.

Think of the many ways university athletics can be corrupted. A favoured athlete can be offered a summer sinecure by a businessman who is a fan of the team. Money can be funnelled to star athletes in various ways: part-time non-jobs, gifts, the loan of a car, and so on. The Canadian Interuniversity Athletic Union has strict rules designed to prevent the corruption of sport in this way, but it's tough to keep it clean.

Athletics is treading on dangerous ground when a game or a team playing a major sport becomes symbolic of a university, when competition becomes a matter of prestige, when fans and alumni chime in to demand victory. Then corners can be cut and rules broken, the athletes come under tremendous pressure (some of it self-generated). Result: situations like the 2010 steroid scandal involving members of the University of Waterloo football team.

Perhaps the most corrupting way in which athletics affect universities is that they create, or can create, a group of non-student athletes, people (almost always men, because traditionally it's the men's teams that really matter) who come to university only to play sports, and who fake their courses as much as they can. Universities that offer degrees in education, particularly physical education, can (not all do) offer practical courses that anyone can pass. A few top grades in such courses can offset failures in heavier courses, keeping the athlete's GPA above the magic 2.0, enabling him to stay eligible for intercollegiate athletics for several years. At the end of this, if he drops out without a degree, no one much cares. He's served his purpose.

Why Canadian universities permit this to happen is a mystery. It's different in the United States, where huge sums of money are at stake. An American university team that wins the March Madness national basketball championship can receive millions of extra dollars in alumni donations. This doesn't happen in Canada, where alumni are less generous. When Canadian universities give away their integrity, they do it for free. Fortunately, serious scandals don't happen very often, but the only real preventative is not to have intervarsity athletics at all.

29 Our Universities Are Eurocentric

Students of non-European ancestry dominate many of the largest university campuses in Canada. Many of their families, particularly those from Asia, place a high premium on a university education—something long unattainable in many countries—and urge their children to succeed academically and gain admittance to the best schools and the best programs. When they come to Canadian campuses, however, they often encounter institutions still firmly rooted in Europe and with surprisingly little coverage of the rest of the world. Universities are supposed to be "universal," awakening in their students an awareness of the human condition. They do, but with a decided emphasis on Europe and European legacy countries such as Canada, the United States, and a few overseas colonies.

Decades ago, universities saw themselves as national cheerleaders. They were responsible for ensuring that students were deeply versed in their national history and traditions. Canada was no different in this regard, and our universities placed a great deal of emphasis on their European antecedents. Over time, this resulted in the development of European coverage in the core social science and humanities disciplines, and a surprisingly limited attention to the rest of the world. Universities were a reflection of the European-based societies from which they came.

Then Canada changed. Massive immigration from East Asia, South Asia, the Caribbean, the Middle East, and Africa altered and enriched the

Canadian social fabric. But our institutions shifted only marginally. During the Cold War, Russia got a great deal more attention, and faculty members were hired to study it. When Japan seemed destined to take over as the world's leading economic power, Japan studies grew substantially. And when China replaced Japan as the country of concern, resources shifted to Chinese topics. The ongoing crises in the Middle East and throughout the Islamic world have convinced some institutions to move slowly in this direction. Africa and Latin America, in contrast, have attracted very little attention.

Canadian students of non-European backgrounds can find some coverage of their ancestral homelands, but nothing compared to the resources devoted to European affairs. Many departments would be delighted to expand into new geographical and cultural fields if they get additional funding to do so, but are much more reluctant if they have to eliminate European or North American slots.

Equally, Canadian students of European backgrounds have a limited understanding of global affairs because they have few opportunities to take courses outside the Europe-North America zone. And these students are particularly reluctant to study Asian languages, despite the continuing importance of that part of the world. What's more, few programs require students to take specific courses designed to provide a broad understanding of global affairs and to come to terms with developments in emerging or crisis-filled areas.

Canadian universities must take deliberate and thoughtful steps to catch up with globalization and the rapid developments in the non-European world. It's vital that philosophy students be introduced to philosophical thought from East and South Asian countries, that African political cultures be explained to political science students, that English students be exposed to voices outside the Western canon, and that history students understand how Latin America and the Middle East factor into world affairs. Europe and North America will remain important to Canadian students and will even retain their prominent position. But universities let their students down if they do not make concerted and deliberate steps to shift resources to cover other parts of the world.

30 Engineers Are a Hot-Ticket Item

And they have been since the 1950s and the Cold War space race that sparked the great expansion of the university system. The digital revolution and the search for clean tech solutions to environmental challenges are only two of the many fields where there's a big demand for engineers.

Companies are anxious to hire engineering co-op students and graduates. Those in the top fields—systems design and software engineering are very popular right now—have little difficulty finding work. And as the global science-based economy ramps up—fuelled by the belief that science- and technology-based innovation holds the key to national prosperity—the need for more engineers will continue to escalate.

Engineers have done well over the past sixty years, but never more so than now. Universities will be hard pressed to keep up with the demand, and the supply of qualified and motivated Canadian students is way too low. If assumptions about a link between national wealth and engineering degrees are true, then the country has some catching up to do.

Forty years ago Canada and other Western nations needed well-trained people, particularly from the social sciences and humanities, to run the large national companies, the multinationals and rapidly growing governments. The need for engineers was offset by an equal need for a different professional class. Years of streamlining, downsizing, and outsourcing appear to have lessened the appetite for the well-trained generalist in favour of the highly skilled technical person. Universities have not caught up with the transition.

Neither Canada nor the United States is producing enough engineering undergraduates to meet demand. China, India, South Korea, and other Asian nations are doing much better. The vast majority of PhD candidates in engineering are from other countries. Some stay in Canada and the United States and make great contributions; a growing number return to the economic powerhouses of Asia, where there is great demand for their services.

Canadian schools and universities must do better at attracting senior students to careers in engineering. Other countries have gained a real advantage in the engineering sweepstakes—and a significant portion of Canada's prosperity may be at stake.

 # Business and the University

Business is playing an ever-larger role in Canadian universities. On balance, this is a good and important development. More university training is focused on business-related skills and less on general education. Government grants often require matching funds from business. Successful business leaders have made huge contributions to the top universities, allowing for major expansions in facilities and programming.

Critics have raised legitimate questions about the role of corporations and business leaders in shaping the academic agendas of the campus, accusing them of trying to transform the educational and research functions into feeders for corporations. Business people can be demanding and they often misunderstand the nature and purpose of a university, so the relationships can be very awkward and often tense.

For the past two generations, however, universities have presented themselves as engines of economic development and regional stability. The arguments for major research grants, research facilities, more graduate spots, new programs, and the like are routinely wrapped in promises to enhance training, commercialization, and economic development. These are not new arguments, but they have become more urgent and commonplace in the science-driven innovation economies of the twenty-first century. Students have certainly picked up on the message, and many see a university education as a stepping-stone to prosperity.

Business, government, students, and the general public expect their universities to serve society, and given that the present generation sees this largely in terms of business development and job creation, universities have little choice but to stay engaged.

That's not to say the entire academic enterprise must be turned over to a corporate agenda. Universities also exist as the analysts, critics, and conscience of society. Canada needs more of the critical and provocative assessment of business and the commercial thrust of the modern age. Most of this critique is currently coming from off campus. Working with business does not mean kowtowing to it.

What does it mean to co-operate with corporations? It means paying close attention to employment market needs and adjusting courses and programs to stay current. It means talking to business leaders to discover opportunities for collaborative research and collective problem solving. It means expecting Canadian corporations to pay for their share of the research infrastructure and educational enterprise—universities must not become taxpayer-subsidized supports for business.

In turn, the business community has to pay closer attention to the critiques and analysis offered by university, to respond to the moral imperatives of our age, and to commit itself to solving shared problems.

Universities will not lose their autonomy and independence if they co-operate with the corporate sector and engage with it as serious players in the educational and research enterprises. They will instead maintain relevance, attract more resources, better serve their students, and contribute to the economic development of the country if and when they help businesses succeed.

Canadian universities and corporations do not co-operate particularly well. The places that set the gold standard for collaboration—Silicon Valley, the Boston corridor, Finland, South Korea, Singapore, Taiwan, Hong Kong—do much better. The co-operation is fuelling regional competitiveness and employment. These areas get more money from both the corporate world and government, largely because they are contributing to prosperity. There is a lesson to be learned here, and our universities should learn it.

Do Grade 2 Teachers Need Five Years of Post-secondary Education?

Arguably they don't, but there's more to the issue than this. The education of elementary school teachers is a good example of how universities have been used to raise the professional status of certain occupations.

Readers over the age of sixty will remember the day when most elementary school teachers were women. Regulations differed in each province, but the common requirement for these teachers was high school graduation and one year in Teachers' College. These young teachers could begin a career in their late teens.

It's easy to understand why high school teachers need a university degree (and they usually have one). A Grade 12 physics teacher certainly should have a good training in physics (though not all of them do). But why does a Grade 7 teacher need a degree in anything? Surely the first requirement for a teacher at that level is a love of children, and that can't be learned.

But these teachers of the past, often admired and romanticized, were exploited. Because of their short training period, and because the majority were women and non-unionized, salaries were very low and pensions tiny. This, and not necessarily any love of the job, was why many teachers taught for forty-five years, hoping their savings would last after they were forcibly retired at sixty-five.

The road to professionalization began in the 1950s, with unionization and collective bargaining. Higher salaries meant that more men chose to be elementary teachers, and this in turn led to a stronger union. One way to boost the status and pay of teaching was to push for higher academic requirements, a drive that coincided with the government's wish to have a more highly educated population.

And so, in the 1960s, the provinces began to require elementary teachers to have Bachelor's degrees. The requirement was not retroactive, but since their salaries depended on their level of education, all but the oldest began to take extension courses to complete a degree. The next step was the Master of Education degree, which put teachers in an even higher salary bracket (the current difference between the salary of a teacher with four years' education and one with six, at the top rank, can be as much as $15,000). A Master's degree in science or arts would have had the same effect, but hardly any teachers took these degrees.

Nowadays education requirements for teachers vary widely across Canada. In some provinces, three undergraduate years plus a year of teacher training is the minimum; in others it's four years plus one or even two years of teacher training. Some have an "integrated" degree, where teaching and other requirements are completed in four years. Add the MEd—which usually comes later after some time in the classroom—and the total can range from four to six or even seven years—the same as a doctor, and more than a lawyer.

Sure, teaching is a tough job that requires a high level of skill, but does a four-year arts degree with a major in English, followed by a year of teacher training, impart this skill? It's hard to think that a Grade 2 teacher needs as much training as a physician does, and the logical explanation is simply the urge to professionalize what used to be a respected but ill-paid job. Teachers have accomplished this brilliantly. Whether it benefits the students or the general public is a different matter.

33 The Science Tsunami

It may seem extraordinary, but four out of five of all the scientists who ever worked are alive today. Think about that number, and think about all the stuff they are churning out. As late as the 1950s, science was a small field, occupied by researchers working on fairly broad and fundamental problems. Now research work has increasingly been split into small and esoteric inquiries. The total volume of research output overwhelms anyone attempting to stay abreast of new developments. We are staring a scientific tsunami in the face.

It will be magnified by the rapid growth of scientific work in China, India, and eventually the Middle East and Africa. The world is already awash in research papers, grant applications, new theories and ideas, and laboratories. What will it be like in twenty years, when scientific output has doubled and doubled again?

This flood of science hides some brilliant, life-changing work, some potentially dangerous discoveries, a great deal of career-building activity, and a tiny amount of bogus and fraudulent nonsense. How do we tell good from bad, useful from dangerous, legitimate from garbage? Commonly, science runs well ahead of legal and moral concerns, as with the use of gender-based abortions to remove female fetuses, new forms of genetic testing, and the misuse of computer science discoveries by criminals.

The scientists we work with are dedicated scholars, as devoted to their studies as historians and literary researchers are to theirs. Quite a lot of their work fails any real test of relevance and practicality (just like the humanities), but the scientific community has nonetheless done a great deal to convince governments that their work is worthy of more and continuing support.

It's true, the world needs more science, but it needs even more scientific understanding. The explosion of research has overwhelmed our capacity to know and understand what is coming out of the laboratories and field research. The world needs more scientific communicators, more practitioners of the scholarship of synthesis.

We need more people who can wade through the piles of research papers to find the gems that truly illuminate and the trends that can change our lives. We need more awareness of science, more understanding of the impact of new discoveries. And we need, perhaps, less of the original laboratory work that already vastly outstrips our collective capacity to understand and to use effectively.

The new scientist will be a well-trained generalist, able to sift through scientific debris to find the occasional gem, and determined to share the best discoveries with the public, government, and industry. Scientific research must continue, for much depends on improving our understanding of the world. But we need a new type of scientist to save us from drowning in the scientific deluge.

34 The Public Just Doesn't Get Academic Research

Frantz Fanon wouldn't get a Social Sciences and Humanities Research Council grant, and Thomas Edison would be turned down by the Natural Sciences and Engineering Research Council award. So, at least, goes the mantra of critics of academic research.

The Tri-Council agencies, and their close partner, the Canada Foundation for Innovation, sponsor millions of dollars-worth of research each year, supporting faculty members in curiosity-based research programs with one of the best-funded and most academically sound granting arrangements in the world. Those less fond of the system argue it is tilted towards careerist and disciplinary pursuits and is not well suited to supporting problem solving and the general interests of the public at large.

Is the charge fair? Frantz Fanon, a psychiatrist from Martinique, published on the colonial experience from the perspective of the colonized peoples. His books—more argument and even polemic than well-researched analysis—sold many copies, sparked intellectual and political ferment throughout the developing world, and revolutionized world politics in the process. Edison, among the most practical and successful inventors of all time, introduced radical technological changes, backed by strong commercial applications. He would have been the poster child for innovation strategies had he lived in the twenty-first century, but his experimental approaches were more hit-and-miss than systematic—"99 per cent perspiration, 1 per cent inspiration." These people, and many others, were able to generate ideas, innovations, and inventions of enormous importance without help from any university.

This sort of thing still happens. Private companies—the Xerox Laboratory is a prime example, but Canadian firms such as Research In Motion, Open Text, and (before its disastrous fall) Nortel—have also produced great original research. And non-academic think-tanks continue to produce useful commentaries, like those supported in Canada by the Fraser Institute, the North-South Institute, the Centre for International Governance Innovation, the Canada West Foundation, Public Policy Forum, and the C.D. Howe Institute. So—the argument goes—solid, practical, relevant work can be done outside the academy. Why then bother with all of the funding for mainstream academic work?

Having received Tri-Council funding on several occasions, it would be hypocritical for us to turn on agencies that have supported us, and thousands of other Canadian researchers, over the years. We have no desire to do so in any case. In the heyday of government-sponsored research funding—the 1970s and 1980s—the system really was curiosity-driven and faculty-focused. But then the academy heard mounting complaints about "irrelevant" scholarship—the Reform Party of Canada used to routinely try to embarrass the government by publicizing seemingly frivolous research grants—and adjusted accordingly.

The Social Sciences and Humanities Research Council faced the toughest road, largely because funding was so short (fewer than 30 per cent of applicants receive funding in the regular competitions). The Natural Sciences and Engineering Research Council and the Canadian Institutes of Health Research made the transition more readily, partly because there's less public criticism of science and technology than of the arts. It's hard for the average person on the street to complain about a complex project on string theory, but easy to pontificate about the folly of spending tax dollars on studies of "Wartime Shakespeare in a Global Context," "Things in the mind: Cognitive Psychology in the Later Middle Ages," or "Manuscripts and the Forms of Middle English Literary Texts," to pick three examples at random from the 2009 awards.

All the funding agencies, however, have adjusted their programs to include greater community engagement—more partnerships with business, government agencies, and community groups, and a strong emphasis on sharing research results with the public. Research relationships with indigenous groups have been turned on their head to ensure a greater and more constructive impact on Aboriginal communities.

Universities never claimed to be the only places where new ideas would be generated. They never claimed that all research should be handled on campuses. Indeed universities have routinely embraced radical, creative, and innovative thinkers from outside the academy. The writings and discoveries of non-academics routinely show up on academic reading lists. Academic research is deliberately different than the free-flowing, open-ended exchange of ideas and insights that occurs in free and democratic societies. Scholars test ideas and concepts, follow clearly articulated and reproducible methods, and subject their results to rigorous peer review before publication, with the expectation that their work will stand the text of time.

A robust and open society takes its ideas and innovation wherever they are found. Academics are a substantial part of the research puzzle, producing original ideas, testing concepts, improving upon and refining ideas, and exploring new ways of knowing and explaining the natural and human worlds. But they share the public space with many others, from journalists to government agents, researchers in think-tanks, and members of the general public. Fanon, Edison, and many others changed the world for the better—as did countless university researchers who used their institutional base to both address relevant and time-sensitive questions and to explore topics derived from their imagination.

IV
Do Canadian Universities Work?

Putting Bums on Seats Is Crucial

Over the last thirty years, two forces have combined to cause a crisis for many universities. First, in many parts of the country the number of high school students levelled off and then declined. Second, it turned out that not every student who graduated from high school *wanted* to go to university.

In the Maritime provinces there were not enough students to stock the region's many universities—which include some of the country's finest and most attractive institutions. Meanwhile, in Alberta, high school graduates weighed the prospect of four years of study against the high wages of the oil patch. The choice between thirty dollars an hour and Derrida turned out to be a no-brainer for many eighteen-year-olds, and quite often they chose construction over deconstruction.

What's more, even if the young choose differently, the demographics are alarming for universities: in Saskatchewan and Manitoba the number of high school graduates is declining rapidly, as it is in most of Ontario outside the Greater Toronto Area, and in much of British Columbia outside the lower mainland. Put simply, the flow of well-trained and highly motivated high school graduates is slowing at a time when universities need steady or expanding numbers to meet their always-rising costs.

These realities have created a serious challenge, with universities launching aggressive marketing campaigns to attract students—increasingly *any* students—to come to campus.

Universities desperate for warm bodies have had no choice but to go down the grade scale, even though they all know that these students are at academic risk from the beginning. Research has shown consistently that students who are below average (in Ontario, 80 per cent now) in their high school studies face serious difficulties in university. But universities need full classrooms to pay the bills. At least one university (Brandon) will admit any person with a high school diploma—period. And if that standard proves too high, applicants can wait until they are twenty-one years old and then qualify as mature students.

Knowing that university was within relatively easy grasp was not always good enough for many students and parents. They wanted—and demanded—access to a university education close to home. This is why the Greater Toronto Area has a stunning shortage of university spaces, predicted to reach 75,000 within the next few years. Ontario has plenty of extra spots, in Thunder Bay, Windsor, St. Catharines, Brantford, North Bay—all homes to respectable universities. But the pressure on the government to expand opportunities close to home has put pressure on York and Toronto to develop feeder campuses, convinced Trent to open a facility in downtown Toronto, has Milton negotiating with Wilfrid Laurier University on the development of a new campus, and convinced Lakehead to open a branch in Orillia.

But think of this nationally for a second. Stellar universities—Bishop's, St. Francis Xavier, Mount Alison, and Acadia—are desperate for students and would happily take in hundreds from the GTA. So would Lakehead, Nipissing, Brandon, Regina, Saskatchewan, and Manitoba. But instead of working as a national network, and moving students to where the spaces are to be found, governments understand the imperative of the new post-secondary order: parents and students demand a spot close to home.

And so the Canadian university system is expanding in a few places and contracting or struggling in others. The Toronto universities are bursting at the seams, and campuses within relatively easy commuting distance are attracting a sizeable overflow. Alberta is taking up the slack through four-year degree programs at Mount Royal College in Calgary and Grant McEwan College in Edmonton. British Columbia has converted urban university colleges (Malaspina, Kwantlen, Fraser Valley, Emily Carr) to university status (Vancouver Island University, Kwantlen Polytechnic University, University of the Fraser Valley). At the other extreme, places such as Memorial's Cornerbrook campus, the University of New Brunswick at Saint John and St. Thomas in New Brunswick, UPEI on Prince Edward Island, the smaller University of Quebec campuses, Winnipeg, Brandon, Regina, UNBC, and the like struggle to attract enough students to meet their needs.

Even if they can come up with the right number of first-year students, many of these institutions are admitting significant numbers with very low likelihood of succeeding. This situation will only worsen in the coming years, as the numbers of high school graduates in outlying regions continue to fall and as their cohort in key urban centres continues to grow.

The end result of all this is that recruiting has emerged as a growth industry in Canada. Universities and specialized programs now spend hundreds of thousands of dollars wooing students (and their parents) and trying to influence guidance counsellors. Large university and college fairs are held in major centres. Recruiters visit virtually every high school of substantial size in the country. The elite schools make special visits to selected high schools—"selected" being a euphemism for institutions with lots of wealthy and well-educated young people. Private schools are particularly attractive recruiting grounds. Schools in working-class districts or immigrant settlement areas rarely get the same attention. Firms like the Canadian recruitment company EZRecruit use new technologies to personalize university pamphlets and to provide "personal" contact between the university and students.

How can universities avoid this crisis? The federal and provincial governments, supported by private donors, could step in with special travel awards to cover the additional costs of attending university out of province—but this would probably have little effect. It's more likely that in the next ten years or so, some universities will be forced to close or dramatically restructure themselves. This is already occurring in elementary and high schools, and universities will be next.

Change is certainly on the horizon. Some freestanding institutions will likely be merged into a provincial or regional university system, if only to save administrative costs. Some will change from degree-granting status to serving as local access points for first- and second-year students only. Others, seeking to stay independent and relevant, will drop their claims to comprehensiveness and switch to serve specialized academic and professional markets. This, in fact, is the most positive and logical outcome. But since it likely entails adopting a polytechnic approach to post-secondary education—merging university and college programming—it will be fought bitterly by faculty, students, and the institutions at large.

Strong, deliberate action is required, but we're more likely to see a process of grudging, step-by-step change, a process that will only add to the costs, time, and difficulty of aligning Canada's post-secondary resources with the needs, aspirations, and requirements of the country.

36 Coming Your Way: Closing Campuses

Nelson, BC—one of Canada's most picturesque communities, immortalized in Steve Martin's 1986 film *Roxanne*—has another claim to fame. It's one of the few communities in this country, possibly the only one in modern times, to have its university shut the doors.

The university was Notre Dame, a Roman Catholic institution begun in 1951 as a junior college, and chartered by the provincial government as a private university in 1963. At its height it had 2,000 students—a respectable number for a young institution. In the 1970s student numbers began to decline. It was downgraded to a branch college of the University of Victoria in 1977, and in 1984 was closed altogether.

Some say Notre Dame failed because its union activities made it too radical for the provincial government, but the real problem was that there weren't enough students to maintain it. Nelson's population was only about 9,100 in 1981 and it was not growing. It simply could not sustain even a modest-sized university. And the economically weak and sparsely populated Kootenay region lacked the population to produce the students—even at a time when the rest of the province's universities were growing rapidly.

The community struggled to rebuild the university. The buildings were reincarnated as a campus of Selkirk College and later as the David Thompson University Centre. When those failed, it operated briefly as an ESL training centre, catering largely to Japanese students. A group of enthusiasts tried to revive Notre Dame once more in the 1990s, operating as a people's collective, offering a handful of courses to a small number of students. This idealistic experiment foundered quickly when the other universities refused to accept its courses for transfer credit.

Canadians would do well to heed the Nelson-Notre Dame story, for the same thing is likely to happen in other places over the next couple of decades. The process won't be fun to watch, for nothing agonizes a small community like the loss of well-paid white-collar jobs and the exodus of local kids and students with money in their pockets. But it is inevitable, for try as universities and their supporters might to stay afloat, significant parts of Canada are running out of students. And without enough students universities will have to close.

They won't go down without a fight. Students—and especially faculty and civic boosters—will defend their universities to the end. In 2009 the New Brunswick Commission on Higher Education recommended, as part of a sweeping and imaginative package, that the University of New Brunswick at Saint John campus combine with the local community college to form a polytechnic. The campus community was horrified. Mass protests erupted and speakers denounced the scheme. The provincial government backed down. UNBSJ, while experiencing serious enrolment challenges, lives on—for now.

Universities can't afford to ignore the "baby bust." Major institutions and those in larger centres are pretty safe for a generation or more. But in small town Canada—including Atlantic Canada, much of Quebec, Ontario (except the GTA), Manitoba, and Saskatchewan (except for First Nations), and the interior of BC—a demographic time bomb is ticking away. Public institutions are generally less at risk than private universities, but even government campuses can only be subsidized for so long.

The declining population of young people can be seen in elementary and high school closures. Yes Toronto, there are cities in your country where they are closing schools for lack of students—in the Prince George BC school district, fourteen were closed in 2002 and 2003, and another eleven are currently threatened. This negative wave is moving steadily towards the universities.

The Maritime provinces are already feeling the pinch of falling rates of childbirth in the 1980s and 1990s. Universities have reacted—their survival instinct is strong—by lowering admission standards, aggressively recruiting international students, reducing faculty numbers, and cutting back wherever possible. But belt-tightening and streamlining can only go so far. At some point—likely within the next twenty years—a number of Canadian universities will be closed, as they are already being closed in Japan and Taiwan, with their aging populations. Communities will protest and will gain temporary reprieves. But the inevitable can be delayed only so long.

37 University Education Should Be Coordinated Nationally

Can anything be done to prevent universities closing? There is one solution, but it will test the capacity of Canadian institutions to collaborate and the ability of provincial systems to operate in the national interest.

There are just too many spaces in some parts of the country and not enough in others. Ontario is feverishly adding thousands more—20,000 college and university spots in 2010 alone, or more than the capacity of the entire New Brunswick university system. British Columbia has created thousands of new spaces in the lower mainland, and Alberta created spaces largely by converting community colleges to universities.

The solution is simple. We must deflect applications from overcrowded universities to those with space. Stop adding capacity in the big cities and direct students to unused spots in other areas. Provide a little money towards travel costs. Publicize the opportunities across the country. Ensure guidance counsellors advise students of the full range of educational options in Canada. If an Ontario student, university eligible, applies to Toronto, Queen's, and Western, and fails to make the cut, offer her a spot at Nipissing or Windsor. Even better, encourage her to consider universities in another province.

Here's how it would work. Instead of receiving three rejections, she gets a letter listing all the Canadian universities willing to accept her, which are then free to contact her. The pain of being turned down by her first choices is alleviated when she is courted by several attractive universities she hadn't considered. A student who applied to UBC, Victoria, and Simon Fraser ends up at the University of Saskatchewan. Another from Mississauga enrolls at St. Mary's in Halifax. A third, unable to get into the University of Alberta, Lethbridge, or Calgary opts to attend Memorial University of Newfoundland. They all discover different parts of the country and get the education they want.

But don't hold your breath. Canadian students do not like to leave home and—for reasons of finances and family bonds—many parents are not happy to see them go, at least at this stage of their lives. Even worse, an exercise like this would require an unprecedented level of inter-provincial co-operation. Have we seen much of this lately? Alas, an excellent chance to match student demand with university supply probably will not happen. Without the national will to operate our universities as a federal system the inevitable will happen—sooner or later, some Canadian universities are going to close.

Governing the University

University senates have been compared to "letting the lunatics run the asylum." It's a common cliché that reflects the general view of academic governance. Is it fair? Only partly.

Universities have two governing bodies (sometimes with different names): a board of governors and a senate. The first controls financial, property, and similar issues, and is ultimately responsible for the well-being of the university. The second controls academic matters.

The board of governors is a mix of appointees (often by government) and elected faculty, student, and staff representatives. The senate is controlled by elected faculty members, with significant student representation, and is responsible for making all the key academic decisions: program approvals and changes, entrance requirements, academic penalties, schedules, examination rules, and on and on. They have many committees and sub-committees that award scholarships and honorary degrees, hear student appeals, act as disciplinary tribunals, and carry out many other duties. Joint board/senate committees serve as hiring committees for new presidents and senior administrators.

Senates can provide sound academic advice. They review programs for rigour and intellectual substance. They attend to accreditation requirements and strive to ensure cultural and theoretical breadth. They hold the administration's feet to the fire—usually in a collegial and co-operative way. They set, in other words, the intellectual standards and culture for the entire university. Senate debates can be vigorous and sometimes nasty, but they can also be useful. Universities must have senates, and a constructive and able senate can do much to enhance the quality of the institution and the student experience.

But senates can also be ineffective and can slow the work of the university. They can be dominated by people with an axe to grind—particularly faculty unions or students focused on a small number of issues. They often move very slowly and unproductively, devoting huge amounts of time and paper to minor academic administrative matters. At their worst they become battlegrounds between faculty and the administration, straying off academic and into management issues. The amount of high-quality debate about truly academic issues is generally small. The committee structure can be overwhelming: to change the requirements for a course in sociology, for example, the change must be approved by the sociology department (and maybe a curriculum subcommittee too), an arts faculty council, the curriculum committee of the senate, and finally by the whole senate. That's a lot of time spent by highly educated people to decide a simple matter.

Senates need to be reformed rather than eliminated. They vary widely in quality and effectiveness from institution to institution, often reflecting the respect given to the body by the administration and vice versa. A more specific mandate—focusing on high-level issues such as medium- and long-term planning, new programs, campus life, and the like—would be useful, with more detailed matters delegated to other levels of the collegial process. The committee structure needs to be streamlined.

Senates should be learning bodies, where the university discusses and debates its place within the region, nation, and world. There are many forces swirling around universities—commercialization of research, role of private donors, demographic change, and the shifting expectations of students and parents. University faculty and students have a great deal to contribute to the understanding of how these influences will affect universities. Senates should be the embodiment of the intellectual and research-based contributions of the academy.

Want to focus attention on this issue? Put a cost on the operation of these systems—in faculty and staff time for preparation and meetings—and then decide if the shockingly high expenditure is worth the money.

We Should Abolish the Three-Year Degree

When is a university degree not really a degree? When it is a three-year degree! Universities are big on standards, which are supposed to be clear, precise, and uniform. But not all degrees are alike, even BAs and BScs.

How does a three-year degree fit in? Four years of advanced academic study is the standard for undergraduate education in North America, but in Canada, thousands of students graduate with a BA or a BSc degree after three years at university. Technically the four-year and three-year degree are not the same, but not many graduates point this out in their resumes. For most people, a three-year BA equals a four-year BA, though it involves only three-quarters as much work.

The three-year university course was traditionally a "general" degree, while the four-year course was usually an "honours" degree. Students who wanted a general education went for three years, while those aiming at a specialization—graduate school, for instance—went for four. But the logic of this has been lost over the years. In many institutions, the three-year degree is just part of the fabric of academic life, acknowledged as a lesser accomplishment, but tolerated as useful.

But be careful not to typecast the three-year student. Some of the best students in university graduate after three years, heading for medical school, law school, or other professional or career objective. At some universities, including the University of New Brunswick, students accepted into certain advanced programs receive a full BA after one year of study. For these top students, a three-year degree is a preparation, a stepping-stone for a professional degree.

At the opposite end of the scale the three-year degree is a default, the opt-out option for students unwilling or unable (often because of lack of money) to complete a four-year degree. It's particularly popular with older and part-time students who have to work to support themselves, and who may take four or five years to accumulate three years worth of credits. The three-year graduate can also be someone looking for a very general and non-specialist education.

But there have been some fairly disreputable three-year degrees too. One Canadian institution offered a degree that let students pick any ninety credit hours (thirty courses) from the calendar. The idea was to allow a student who was interested in, say, anthropology, to take every anthropology course the university offered—something that was not otherwise possible. A few students did this, but the vast majority took as many first-year courses as they could fit into their timetables, with emphasis on athletics (the university gave credit for athletic skills, and the degree was popular with athletes). The degree was distinctly third rate, did neither the university nor the students any credit, and after a couple of decades was abandoned.

Many reputable universities elsewhere in the world do offer three-year degrees, however. Most students in Australia and New Zealand graduate after three years, as they used to do in Hong Kong, which has very high entrance requirements. The concern about the three-year degree in this country rests as much with the quality of high school education as it does with the university experience. The sorry fact in Canada is that given the unreliability of secondary education, three years is simply not enough to ensure that university students get the skills, experience, knowledge, and maturity that they require. Canadian universities should take a close look at their three-year credential and decide if it meets the standards and needs of the twenty-first century.

40 Universities and Colleges Are Fighting Tooth and Nail

Universities and colleges in Canada should be natural allies. They have a great deal in common, serve the same governments and public, and play crucial roles in ensuring Canadian competitiveness. But they just don't get along.

The public rarely sees the tensions and difficulties that have slowed innovation in the system for decades. Colleges find universities arrogant, aloof, pretentious, and far too academic (that is, non-practical). Universities see colleges as unscholarly, non-academic (that is, having low standards), overly practical and too concerned with meeting employers' needs. The public and guidance counsellors (most of whom are university graduates) clearly see university degrees as more prestigious than college diplomas. Governments, following the public's lead, favour them. Not many colleges have expensive and architecturally impressive buildings. Pragmatism is the college way.

Universities and colleges can and must collaborate. In many ways combining university education and college training is ideal. Some students are clearly destined for university; others are best suited for college. But a substantial group would benefit from a combined university-college program.

Many possibilities exist, including two-plus-two arrangements (two years of college and two years of university), college post-graduate certificates and, more rarely, integrated college-university programs (four- or five-year programs producing a diploma and a degree). And some are operating now: Guelph-Humber, McMaster-Mohawk (collaborative Bachelor of Science of Nursing and Bachelor of Technology programs); Seneca-York; nursing programs in Saskatchewan; and several BC collaborations.

Growing rivalries will exacerbate the challenges. In Ontario, some colleges have been authorized to offer degrees. In Alberta, Grant McEwan and Mount Royal have degree-granting authority. British Columbia converted a number of colleges to university-colleges and then to non-research universities (one, University College of the Okanagan, became a branch of the University of British Columbia). Universities, for their part, are shifting to more practical approaches and more employment-focused degrees and diplomas.

College-university collaborations would improve efficiency, career readiness, and responsiveness to market trends in the post-secondary sector. But major movement here is unlikely. Faculty at both universities and colleges will fight it. Institutional autonomy works against effective partnerships, as do the competing cultures of colleges and universities. If only universities would learn to respect the colleges, and the colleges would stop longing to become universities.

The lack of collaboration produces losers and no winners. Students have fewer well-developed study and career options. Governments pay too much for duplicate programs of studies. Employers have trouble getting the workers they want. And the Canadian economy ends up with a widening gap between available jobs and trained and ready workers. It's truly unfortunate that colleges and universities cannot overcome their differences.

41 The Perfect University System

Canada's university system—or, more properly, its weakly connected network of universities—is impressive in many ways. It's not the best in the world, although it's better than most Canadians believe. But no national university system is perfect. In our view, the ideal system would combine the best characteristics of many different national systems. Here, from around the world, are some examples of what an ideal system would be like.

Utility and impact of the nation's university system: Singapore offers strong coordination and clear planning in academic programming and has produced a tightly coordinated and well-managed system that benefits from the country's tiny size. Kudos also go to the European Union for attempting to regularize and coordinate its academic activities. If only Canada could be so bold.

Impact on the nation's future: Nowhere are universities seen as integral to their country's future more than in Israel and South Korea. The nations' economic, social, cultural, and political vitality seem tightly linked to the success of their university systems.

Academic diversity: The United States has more than 3,000 colleges and universities. There is something for everyone within this network of public and private, religious and secular, large and small, urban and rural institutions. Other countries, notably Japan, have moved in a similar direction, but the fascinating complexity of the American system makes it truly attractive.

Students' work ethic and study habits: China's rigorous standards make it hard to get into the universities and just as hard to get out. Students have a great deal riding on the outcome. In only a few places—Vietnam is an example—is a university education held in such high esteem.

Academic excellence: Germany gets many things right, and academic excellence remains a key achievement of the nation's university system. Academic standards are high, students work hard, and professors achieve a great deal. Hong Kong is doing a very good job in this regard as well.

Commitment to historic traditions and values: The United Kingdom values its academic traditions (less so in the new polytechnics) and sets the gold standard for attention to the past. Few places pay such homage to academic tradition.

Campus culture and social environment: American elite liberal arts colleges provide students with an out-of-class experience without parallel in the world. The combination of residence life, social activities, sports, and even campus food makes for a university lifestyle that is often the highlight of the students' lives.

Intervarsity athletics: American big-league universities do this better than anyone and produce loyalty and excitement on campuses unmatched in the world. In many cases, the national reputation of the university rests on the performance of its football and basketball teams.

Student participation in campus sports and activities: Japanese students often sign up for many different sports and activities and see campus clubs as being an integral part of their university experience. The swirl of student activities gives Japanese universities a remarkable vibrancy and sense of energy.

Impact of faculty research: While big-name universities in the United States and other places do extremely well, Canada does an excellent job of ensuring that faculty members across the country are able to engage in international quality research. Canadian scholars do extremely well and reflect the benefits of the substantial and ongoing investments by provincial and national governments in this field.

Government funding: Hong Kong has the right idea—well-funded and well-managed universities, closely connected to government planning priorities, and without the kind of quality-destroying commitment to access that undermines academic excellence.

Philanthropy: The United States has donor relations down to a fine art and produces hundreds of millions of dollars for academic projects. But keep an eye on developments in the Middle East and India, where many very wealthy people are turning their attentions—and their money—towards post-secondary education.

Academic-business relations: East Asian universities are doing more and are doing it better. For our money, Taiwan and South Korea do this the best, with South Korea making an increased effort to develop its connections in this vital area.

Campus environments: The top European universities combine historic architecture and modern functionality in a way that should (but oddly does not) inspire architects responsible for the new institutions. Check out the Catholic University of Leuven (Belgium) for a real piece of academic eye candy.

Student activism: Campuses that bubbled with turmoil in the 1960s and 1970s have turned sadly quiet. But there are still pockets of dissent and courage, particularly in places like South Korea (which is calming down) and Iran (where students have been central in pro-democracy and anti-government movements).

Attention to academic contributions: Scandinavian governments—with Norway in the lead—are extremely respectful of academic contributions and expect scholars to make solid and sustained contributions to national policy. The government pays attention when they do.

V

The View from the Front of the Class

Students Aren't Interested in Book Learning

Universities tell themselves many things to get them through the night. One of them is that most of their students are interested in the material they are studying. You don't have to spend much time in a classroom, or around students to realize that this is partly a fantasy. Many students—just how many is difficult to determine, but it's probably a majority—have no deep interest in the material presented in class, or in what they read while preparing essays. They are willing to listen and be entertained, but they are not deeply engaged. To put it bluntly, they are not interested in book learning.

By book learning we mean the printed word, the storehouse of knowledge that has accumulated in books in the thousands of years since writing was invented, later in journals and newspapers, and now in electronic form. All disciplines are based on it: some—like history, English, and philosophy—almost totally. If you are going to get the most out of the study of political science, for example, you have to read—and read extensively. Students who come out of university knowing only what they have been told in class (assuming they know even that), and what they have researched for their written assignments, have learned only a fraction of what they should know. If they don't read on their own during—and especially after—their college days, they have to a large extent wasted their time.

It's not that no one reads books. Despite the Internet, book sales in Canada are reasonably healthy, or at least they are when the economy is good. Books are being bought and read, but students are not reading books that tell them about their country, the world, current events, past events, science, art, architecture, and politics—in other words, serious non-fiction. The same is true of serious fiction too: it would be interesting to find out how many students in English classes read novels (Michael Ondaatje, not J.K. Rowling) and poetry other than the assigned readings.

The habit of reading is best acquired early, and if young men and women arrive at university in their late teens having never read a serious book other than those a high school teacher forced them to read, they will probably never acquire it, especially if they don't pick it up during the course of their studies.

Students do not even turn to other sources for serious information. Ask a class how many read a newspaper regularly, and see if any hands go up. Usually there is silence, and the same is true of magazines—even *Maclean's*. Nor do they watch news on TV, (though they're not missing much). The problem is particularly acute in the humanities and social sciences, which rely on book learning more than the natural and physical sciences do.

Ask students this question: have you ever gone to the library to get a quotation or fact from a book for a term paper, started to leaf through the book, and become so interested you couldn't put it down,? Very few will say yes, though of course the Internet has made it possible to write term papers without ever going to the library—or for that matter, ever getting out of bed.

There's nothing intrinsically wrong with a lack of interest in book learn-ing. Not everything is for everybody. Some 15 per cent of Canadians have no interest in hockey (yes, it's true), but they don't spend their own and taxpayers' money attending hockey camps. The non-bookish, however, clog the universities. What do they retain from their studies? Most who graduate are more literate than when they went in—no mean accomplishment these days—but they retain little else, and have read as little as possible. Is this why we spend billions on post-secondary education?

Universities have a term these days for the habit of reading: they call it "life-long learning," and it's one of the things they are supposed to instill in their students. Clearly, with a great many students this is not being done, though it's not clear how the universities are supposed to do it. You can lead a horse to the river, but you can't make him drink, especially if he has no taste for water.

43 Students Read Junk

Are university students illiterate? You hear this sometimes from English professors, but it's not true, unless you expand the definition of illiteracy fairly widely. There are few Canadian-born students at Canadian universities who cannot read and write well enough to get through life one way or another, even if they can't read an income tax form. But if what they don't read is depressing enough, take a look at what they do read.

Canadian university book stores don't seem to keep national lists of what students are buying and reading, but American bookstores do, and there's no reason to think that there's much difference in student tastes between the two countries. They watch the same TV shows, and almost certainly read the same books. Here's the January 2010 top ten list at U.S. university bookstores. Notably, four of the top five are tied to movies. Read it and weep.

> 10. *The Gathering Storm.* Do women read this stuff, or is this just
> guy escapist fantasy?

9. *Push.* "Charts the psychic damage of the most ghettoized of inner-city inhabitants." For Oprah fans.

8. *Freakonomics: A Rogue Economist Explores the Hidden Side of Everything.* Such as, "if drug dealers make so much money, why do they still live with their mothers?" A "cultural phenomenon" that's fun reading for a lazy afternoon. This one doesn't depress us.

7. *Pride and Prejudice and Zombies.* "The Classic Regency Romance, Now With Ultraviolent Zombie Mayhem!" Sigh.

6. *What the Dog Saw, and Other Adventures.* Malcolm Gladwell's latest. Like Freakonomics, fun to read.

5. *Precious.* The movie tie-in of Push.

4. *The Time Traveller's Wife.* Romantic science fiction.

3. *Eclipse.* Stephanie Meyer's latest in a hugely popular series about vampires.

2. *Superfreakonomics.* The sequel to Freakonomics.

1. *The Lost Symbol.* The sequel to The Da Vinci Code.

Of course, some students are no doubt buying and reading Marx's *Das Kapital,* Thomas Aquinas' *Summa Theologica,* and *The Diary of Samuel Pepys.* It's just that not enough are buying these books to put them on the best-seller list. That's not the point here. The point is that these are the books that most students are buying, and only three of them are at all serious: 8, 6, and 2, which are pop explanations of modern culture. Of the rest, two (9 and 5) are Oprah-type books, and the other five are simply escapism.

Although the success of almost any book (*Mein Kampf* excepted) should be a reason to celebrate, the thought that anyone over the age of twelve—or heaven forbid, a university student—reads this stuff is seriously depressing.

Why in heaven's name would so many university students want to read a book about vampires, one whose emotional pitch is aimed at twelve-year-old girls? Does adolescence last that long? Apparently it does on campus. The same question can be asked about zombies. Perhaps, like Harlequin Romances, it's the soft-core porn treatment of sexual desire that sells the books and movies. We assume that most buyers of these books at university bookstores are female, and the buyers of the science fiction/fantasy books are male, but we have no way of knowing.

We don't want to beat up on Oprah. She has millions of fans, and her product makes many people feel better about their lives. But her books are entertainment.

The most depressing one on the list is number one, *The Lost Symbol.* Dan Brown's books are simply rubbish. Their plots about the secret cabals of the Roman Catholic Church are stupid beyond belief, and as reviewers have pointed out, they aren't even very well written. Students in search of escape might as well read comic books, which at least don't pretend to be real.

44 Campus Idealism Is Dead and Buried

Remember the youth culture of the 1960s and early 1970s? Students and faculty protested against the war in Vietnam, fought against racial discrimination, had as much sex and drugs as possible, supported full rights for gays and visible minorities, and battled against university administrations they thought were too chummy with the military, business, or the social status quo.

These were heady times for young people. There were sit-ins, teach-ins, be-ins, protests, and office occupations. Some were violent and destructive too, notably at Sir George Williams (now Concordia) University in January 1969. Radical music, Allen Ginsberg's poetry, Tom Robbins' books, and Timothy Leary's drug propaganda rocked university campuses. Then as now the American influence was strong. Students brought their anger and idealism into the classroom where, particularly among the younger professors, they found kindred spirits. Although they were always a minority—most students just wanted to get on with their studies—they made the campuses rock with energy and idealism.

Not any more. Save for some battles over Israeli issues, Canadian universities are pretty staid places. Forget the days when fiery speakers packed lecture halls with passionate students. Now it is Justin Trudeau, an establishment figure if there ever was one, who packs them in. Get Bill Gates or Jim Balsillie on campus and students will turn out in droves. Not too far right, though: the extremely conservative and abrasive Ann Coulter was too much for Carleton University to swallow.

The university teachers who got jobs in the 1960s and the 1970s were schooled in the language of revolution and protests. They weren't all hardlefties by any means, but most were fairly liberal, and some carried a torch throughout their careers for the days when idealism dominated campus life. Those who are still teaching, and the younger colleagues who agree with their views, still struggle to stir up passions—against the war in Afghanistan, mistreatment of First Nations, social conservatism, America, or global warming—but nowadays, except at one or two campuses, without much success.

It's important to remember that the battles of the 1960s were mostly victories. Sexual freedom, anti-discrimination and human rights legislation, support for women, new approaches to First Nations affairs, a less-aggressive approach to overseas war, and so on are the direct result of '60s protests. And universities played a crucial role in the success of one of the most comprehensive social revolutions in history—the women's movement.

Where does that leave universities now? The standard view is that universities are leaders of social change, but this isn't really true. There are faculty and students who tilt against the windmills of the status quo, but they are a minority. Universities are on the whole mainstream institutions, supported by and reflecting the values of the dominant society. As such, they do more to illustrate broad values and assumptions than to challenge them.

We do not live in a radical age, particularly in Canada. Canada is a moderate country, proud of being nice, of avoiding conflict, and of focusing on stability and equality of opportunity. There are pockets of idealism—Native studies programs are a good example, although they have taken a practical turn of late—but our universities are career-building institutions, not cauldrons of radicalism and idealism.

Even in the 1960s Canadian universities were pretty tame places by global standards. Amidst the turmoil most students sought degrees, jobs, and a spot in the middle class. Now, universities are even more mainstream. Faculty care more about career advancement than pushing radical change. Students are preoccupied with practical objectives. Student unions are more likely to work with, rather than against, university administrations.

If idealism is weak or dying, it says more about Canadian society as a whole than it does about the universities. Students should be worried about global warming, but that strikes too close to their quality of life—when we meet the enemy, only to find it's us, it's hard to work ourselves into a righteous frenzy. The calmness and practicality of the university system reflects the high level of comfort most Canadians have with their lives. We don't live in a radical time. We are not seeking major societal change. We have no grand issues. And so universities, reflecting the society in which they exist, have become quiet, even complacent places.

Part-time Student Work and the Beer Index

From time to time we've conducted little experiments in which we ask our classes, by a show of hands, a couple of questions. First, how many work for wages during the academic year, and second, how many work more than ten hours a week. The results are always the same: roughly two-thirds, sometimes more, answer yes to the first, and a quarter or so say yes to the second. Some work twenty hours a week or more while taking a full course load.

This does not include student-parents who, whether they also work for wages or not, must have no spare time at all. We are talking here about students in the traditional age group who attend class fifteen hours a week, do lab work, write essays, study for tests, and also work in bars, restaurants, or similar places.

Why do they do this? For many, it's the desire to avoid graduating with a large student debt. You can hardly blame a student for not wanting to start life owing $25,000 or more. The cost of tuition, room and board, books, and pocket money can be $15,000 a year, and it's tough to find a summer job that will pay that much in four or five months, though some students manage to do so. For others, it's a lifestyle choice: a car, an iPod, or computer games.

What these students miss, however, is one of the greatest gifts that a university can give—leisure time. For undergraduates who do not need to work for wages, even for those in demanding science programs with heavy lab work, there will be many free hours in the week. They can socialize, debate, hang out, join clubs and political societies, sing in the choir, conduct lab experiments on their own, and most of all, they can haunt the library and read. Self-education is a huge part of the university experience. Students who learn only what they hear in class have lost a big chunk of what they should have gained from university, and this is a tremendous pity.

In a way, though, you can hardly blame them. The cost of the lighter side of university life is much greater than it was two generations ago. In the mid 1960s, you could buy a ten-ounce glass of beer in Ontario for fifteen cents, and the minimum wage was $1.50 an hour. That's ten glasses of beer for an hour's work. Now a similar amount of (imported) suds costs about $3, with a minimum wage of about $9 an hour. That's three glasses of beer for an hour's work, disregarding taxes, which are also much higher now. So the "Beer Index," a rough-and-ready guide to the cost of student living, has more than tripled. Forty years ago it was not necessary to make a choice between beer and other expenses. Now it is. No wonder students find they have to work.

Students Are No Longer in Awe of Their Professors

And perhaps this isn't a bad thing. Years ago, university teachers had the image of being highly intelligent but a bit weird: the classic "absent-minded professor." You wouldn't ask them for directions, or how to fix your car, but they certainly knew a lot.

Many graduates from the years before the 1990s remember fondly the erudition, wisdom, and insight of some of their professors. They quoted the Bible or Marx at will, called on a vast storehouse of information, and seemed to have a bibliographic file box fixed to their brains. Students were in awe, amazed that they had so much knowledge at their fingertips. The eighteenth-century poet Oliver Goldsmith said it best:

And still they gazed, and still the wonder grew
That one small head could carry all he knew.

Times have changed. Faculty still know tons of stuff, and most can fill you with as much information as you can hold. The most popular professors are often charismatic lecturers—may it always be thus—or great teachers, but the mystique is largely gone. Students often address their professors by their first names and have clearly taken them down from their pedestals.

The belief in faculty expertise, and in expertise more generally, has been undercut by three elements. First, high school students are encouraged to have and to hold strong opinions, rewarded as much for speaking their mind as for having something to say. Praised for making an effort—"Good job, Susie!"—rather than being right, they are impatient with being corrected.

Second, people born after 1970, those who began to come to university in the 1990s, were not trained to "respect their elders" and other authority figures in the way their parents were. "Never trust anyone over thirty" has had a profound effect on relations between the generations.

The Internet is the other expertise killer. Wikipedia—which many in the university love to hate, but which is actually both useful and mostly accurate—along with Google and the like, are but a few of the Internet tools available to anyone anywhere, including in the middle of classes. Professors can still be knowledgeable and impressive, but the average undergraduate can find a great deal of information—and many answers—with a few keystrokes. It's a whole different ball game in class when instructors find students fact-checking their lectures on laptops.

Specialization is also changing the very nature of academic expertise. Once trained as generalists, with a broad grounding in a discipline, faculty are more and more narrowly focused. Why? Because knowledge is expanding so fast that it's hard to keep up in the broader discipline.

And so the awe is largely gone from the university experience. Faculty are still just as smart, but the classic man or woman of letters—erudite and deeply informed—is increasingly rare. Students are blasé in the extreme. Profs know stuff. They are aggregators of knowledge, facilitators of learning, and mentors extraordinaire. But they are rarely seen as fonts of wisdom and repositories of the knowledge of the ages.

47 The Entitlement Generation Has Changed the Game

A decade ago faculty members at a Maritime university started complaining over coffee about their students' behaviour in class: inconsistent attendance, lack of respect for professors, poor classroom behaviour, litigiousness, and a reluctance to complete assignments. At a meeting with high school counsellors, they asked an obvious question: "what is going on with the current group of students?" The reply was unexpected: "If you think this is bad, wait until you see the Grade 9s that are coming." It's true. Something new and nasty is going on with university students these days, and there's more trouble in store.

Every generation claims that the next one has been coddled and spoiled, but it really may be true this time. There are dozens of explanations for the remarkable freedom, high expectations, and unreasonable demands of today's youth. There's the guilt and the money of two-income families, societal permissiveness, child-centred educational and parenting styles, overwhelming materialism, video games, sexualized media, and on and on.

The changes in the student psyche are not all bad, of course. These "spoiled" students are more assertive, very confident, able and willing to express their opinions, not intimidated by adults and professors, and very sure of themselves.

But they also have a deep sense of entitlement. They expect material well-being and an easy passage through school, university, and work. They expect a great deal from their professors and university staff and can be quite nasty if those expectations are not met. Their evaluations of their profs can be devastating.

They often expect deadlines to be altered, want their explanations accepted without confirmation, and try to insist that course requirements fit their availability to do work. Not all students fit this description, but the general student population has changed.

The entitlement generation had it pretty good at home and in school, and they expect this to continue at university and in the workforce. They are used to parents and other adults responding to their demands and have developed a pretty limitless sense of their future prospects. When these students reach university they bring a lifetime of being celebrated at every turn and of being protected from the realities of life and hardship.

The entitlement students are causing quite a problem on campus, not least by reducing the attractiveness of the classroom and the joy of teaching. The complaining of the most-demanding minority really upsets faculty members, who expect deference—if not respect and awe—from their students.

The university system has adapted in dramatic ways. Check out the food in the cafeteria, the additional facilities in the residences, the greater flexibility of many faculty members, and the declining work demands on the students. These young people, however over-entitled they may be, are the universities' clients, after all, and they have to be kept content, if not completely happy. Universities continue to adapt to the students, perhaps not realizing that responding to the demands for change will fuel even higher expectations.

The entitlement generation seems to be gradually importing the assumptions and demeanour of parenting and the school system into post-secondary education. There is a grave inconsistency between the requirements for academic excellence and professional achievement and the student-pleasing priorities of the youth-centred realities of our time. It remains to be seen what gives first: the standards and requirements of the academy or the expectations and demands of young people.

In other chapters we question whether universities will continue to shape themselves according to student wishes, or whether they will retreat to a more traditional curriculum. History suggests a bet on the university is safe, but a visit to a high school leaves the impression that it's a risky gamble. Youth may well win out—at considerable cost to the universities, the future work force, and the country.

48 Eighteen Is the New Fifteen

We love our students. Honest. If we were writing this in the late 1960s and early 1970s, we might well be complaining about the students' long hair, contempt for authority, and preference for narcotic substances. But times change, and this generation—like all generations—has certain defining characteristics that need to be acknowledged and understood. Students need to know that we have them sussed out a little. Parents need to know that we understand their children. And faculty and staff at university need to see in writing what they live with on a daily basis. What follows has not been researched and is a vast generalization. But it's what we (the authors) think and what we experience.

There's no polite way of saying this: many of today's students, particularly the young men, are not very mature. "Big shock!" scream parents across the country. It's well known that young people today—and my, it makes us feel old to write that—are not as self-reliant and independent as in the past. The reasons for this are many: a child-centred and limited-discipline education system, spoiling by parents, the "everyone's a winner" ethos that has eliminated failure from the lives of many (particularly the well to do), and the high level of creature comforts enjoyed by many in Canadian society.

Whatever the reasons, the outcome is remarkable. University students act younger than ever. Their birth certificates say they are eighteen, but their behaviour and attitude suggest that they are fifteen. They do not show the maturity of their years—and expectations for eighteen-year-olds have not always been particularly high—and some serious problems are emerging. Some young men seem to make particularly bad choices and find themselves in serious difficulties. They do not manage their time well, shirk their responsibilities, and have a problem exercising their freedom. If you do not believe us, ask eighteen-year-old girls, who are often quick to comment on the shortcomings of their classmates on the maturity scale.

We leave this with you to ponder, for the observation is so impressionistic that elaboration would be misleading. First-year students, the classic eighteen-year-olds, are being asked to make huge decisions of great importance to their long-term development. Universities and society at large insist on a high level of independence—young people this age can drive, vote, and join the army—but leave them with little armour at one of the most challenging points in their lives. Academic systems assume and even demand a high level of maturity. If our impression is right—and we are confident that it is—then there's a major disconnect between the world of young adults, particularly the men, and the expectations and processes of the university system.

Getting By on the Bare Minimum of Work

Recently, *The Chronicle of Higher Education* published a report on student study habits in the United States, showing that in 1961 the average student spent twenty-four hours a week studying, whereas now, nearly fifty years later, the figure has declined to fourteen hours.

Universities have always had an unofficial standard: two hours study outside the classroom for every hour inside. A three-hour class should be matched with six hours of studying. We define "studying" fairly loosely, taking into consideration the fact that science students spend many non-class hours in the lab, and that for other students studying simply means reading, as well as writing essays and revising class notes. If you define studying as "all academic activity conducted outside class," the statistic is still alarming, and sad.

For too many students nowadays, studying is limited to the bare essentials—essay writing, a quick flip through some of the readings, and cramming for mid-terms and finals. Faculty complain routinely that students devote too little time to their studies, come to class ill prepared, and make insufficient effort to keep up with the material.

In fairness some study time in the past was spent on mechanical work that is no longer necessary. An on-line library catalogue is much faster than a card index and can be consulted from a residence room. Time formerly spent rewriting sloppy class notes has been freed up by the posting of lecture notes on-line. How many hours have been liberated by word-processing programs and computers? What would a student of today do if given a manual typewriter and the requirement to produce error-free text? (Answer: learn the joys of carbon paper and whiteout.) We should be a little wary of these statistics.

There is a more basic issue here. For a full-time student, university is supposed to be a full-time job. This does not mean just attending all fifteen to twenty hours of lectures, labs, and seminars, although it would be nice if students did even that. It means spending forty-five to fifty hours a week in classes, preparation, research, writing, reading, and thinking. It means learning and using classes as the launching pad for discovery and intellectual enrichment.

Faculty members expect and need students to devote themselves to their studies and to capitalize on the intellectual opportunities of the university—courses and programs require students' full engagement to cover the material. Half measures simply don't wash, and students who don't study, in the broadly defined sense, miss opportunities and diminish their university experience. Faculty concern is not just about students' declining attention to their particular fields. Rather, it's about the increase in the number of students who have little interest in intellectual matters at all.

Here is another of those crucial disconnects, more serious than the number of hours spent studying. Faculty members love to learn. Most adore their jobs because they can spend so much time in intellectual pursuits. They are dismayed by students who neither engage intellectually nor demonstrate curiosity, thus missing the essence of being at university, rejecting the very idea of what it is about. We don't have good statistics yet on what is in students' minds, but the widespread perception is that fewer and fewer of them are participating beyond the bare minimum required for a degree.

We Should Demand More, Not Less, from Our Students

A few years back a university was developing a marketing plan aimed at incoming students. "It's All About You!!!" the promotional material sang—sending precisely the wrong message. University is not all about students, or shouldn't be. The current pattern of seeing students as customers, to be cultivated and pampered, is fundamentally wrong.

Universities have stopped expecting an all-out effort from students.

While failure is still a possibility at university, in many programs passing does not require the same effort it did a few decades ago. Much of the responsibility for success has shifted from the student to the institution. Universities now offer all measure of remedial assistance, disability supports, accommodations, and exemptions. Professors often shy away from high-level demands because they generate student anger, lengthy student appeals, and all manner of other challenges. Did any Canadian university have a "Student Success Centre" in 1960? If so we haven't heard of it. In 1960, student success was up to the student.

This doesn't happen in other areas of high-level performance. Coaches don't exempt players from practice because they are having a hard day. They don't mollycoddle and cajole, nor do they entice and gently encourage. They bellow and demand. They exist as a presence in athletes' minds even when they are not around. No one tries to make sure the athletes had a good time and felt comfortable with their effort. The goal is winning; the requirement full-out effort. It's the same in the performing arts. Top ballet and music teachers press and insist. Top-level sports and high-quality music and dance require total effort and commitment—from both those in training and those training them.

Why don't we see such commitment in other disciplines? To stick to the sports analogy, university has shifted from being an elite athletic competition to an intramural event. It's like giving the participants in water polo—an intense and brutal sport, requiring great strength, speed, and stamina—inner tubes to help them float. It's fun, easy to learn, doesn't require maximum effort and allows everyone to play—but it doesn't produce champions. Instead, it produces graduates who have been encouraged, celebrated for small successes, and permitted to operate in a world of false competition and minimal achievement.

Champions do exist in small numbers in Canada but in much higher numbers in China, Korea, Japan, and India. The top graduates of these countries—and elite American schools—have the attitudes and abilities that push their nation forward. Canadian graduates too often feel better about themselves and their accomplishments than they should. A cruel, competitive world, one that rewards hard-driving winners and casts aside those with a sense of entitlement, awaits.

In Praise of Single Parents

Many students work hard, but there's a special category we'd like to mention: single parents, almost all of them women, who attend classes, care for their children, and sometimes work part or full time.

We stand in awe of a student who can get up in the morning, take her kids to school or daycare, come to campus, attend lectures, take notes, work on term papers, study, come home, pick up the kids, cook dinner, leave the kids with a grandparent or other baby-sitter, work a shift somewhere, come back and study, then get up the next morning and do it all over again. If the student can't manage a full five-course load, she will either take summer courses, or if she works full time in the summer, her undergraduate career will be six years or more instead of four.

We even knew (and we hope our surprise is not sexist), a man who did this—a young fellow left with a two-year-old daughter. He attended classes full time, earned good grades, worked long shifts as a bouncer in a bar, found care for his daughter, and is now a successful lawyer. Good for him.

The motivation of these students is obvious—a desire to care for their children and to provide a better life for themselves and their families—and most of them show tremendous dedication to their studies. Few, in fact, ask for special privileges or even draw attention to their family circumstances. They are not looking for sympathy or academic concessions, even though most faculty make accommodations when family circumstances warrant.

Some of these student/parents live close to grandparents who can look after the children during school hours. Others find subsidized spots in university daycare centres, though these have lengthy waiting lists. Still others share the responsibilities with other students, usually through elaborate timetable negotiations. In a real pinch some parents bring babies and toddlers to campus, worried about disrupting the lectures but desperate not to miss classes.

Many single parents have little money. Student loans and, if they are lucky, access to family housing on campus, help pay the bills—all the while adding to debt. Many of these students, of course, have to find part-time jobs to supplement their income, adding to child-care challenges, detracting from homework time, and compounding the difficulties of attending school. Canada's financial aid requirements have provisions for single parents and their children, but some of this will eventually have to be paid back. While most Canadians are comfortable with the idea of a young adult making do on a heavy overdose of macaroni and cheese, many would be concerned about the single parent student's ability to feed, clothe, and otherwise support her children this way.

Single parents often stand out. They are typically among the most dedicated in class, and they have little time for young adult slackers who do not take advantage of their educational opportunities. They are highly motivated, if only because of the personal and financial sacrifice that they and their children are making. The single parents are often perennially tired, exhausted by the constant balancing act, and the pressures of combining parenting and academic studies.

So, save a special cheer at convocation for the single parents crossing the stage. They are often identified by the loud "Way to go, Mom!" yell that comes from the audience. Rest assured that the faculty members on the stage, aware of the challenges of the single moms and dads, are cheering too. As for us, we'd like to give them a medal.

Eighteen-Year-Olds Control Our Universities

More than thirty years ago, at a university we won't name—oh, what the hell, it was UBC—several physical education students gathered in a student advising area at the beginning of term. They had to declare a major and, since many aspired to be schoolteachers, they were searching for a second "teachable" subject. Three of them, after deep thought, settled on geography. Their rationale? The building where the geography courses were taught was several blocks closer to the gym than the buildings where history and English students studied.

Such shallowness is, we hope, not universal, but the situation exposes a weakness of the Canadian university system. It's clear that Canadian universities are very student-centric, trying to attract and retain as many students as possible. It's also clear that our universities, like Canadian society as a whole, are driven by personal choice more than the needs of society. The idea of acting in the best interests of the province or the country takes a distant back seat to the desire to do what the individual wants to do.

People rarely discuss the implications of these realities. But consider this. Over time, universities respond to student demand. If the students start to bunch up in one or two areas—like psychology in the 1970s, computer science in the 1990s, accounting and business in the past twenty years—there is great pressure to expand course and program offerings. Faculty members in the high-demand fields clamour for more resources, citing unprecedented enrolment figures to back up their requests. Eventually, the number of faculty positions, staff members, and classrooms adjusts to student numbers.

Result: the collective decisions of tens of thousands of eighteen-year-olds—and these students as they work their way through their degrees—determine the shape of the Canadian university system and the expenditure of billions of dollars.

This is fine when the marketplace aligns, in its mysterious way, with the academic interests of university students. In the 1960s and 1970s things aligned, largely because university-educated students were in short supply and jobs were abundant. By the 1980s, the supply and demand curves had separated, particularly at the level of individual programs. So, at times, Canadian universities produced too many schoolteachers, or not enough. The same is true of medical doctors and nurses. Currently the Canadian economy is short of engineers, medical professionals, and other highly technical graduates, while the number of humanities and social science grads is not well matched with career opportunities.

Universities do make choices, largely by regulating entry—there are only so many seats in the classrooms, after all—although even that has proven remarkably elastic in recent years. This, in turn, makes these programs more competitive, allowing departments and faculties to select just the students they want. The other, more open-entry areas end up with a broader cross-section of the incoming population. It's harder to get into engineering than mathematics—programs requiring much the same level of ability and skill—and much easier to get into first-year arts than law school. Interestingly, education programs are among the most difficult to get into across the country, largely because they provide a straight-line route to a comfortable middle-class career.

Of course, when governments have tried to regulate the production of graduates in specified fields they have been sharply criticized and, more often than not, have judged demand incorrectly. Part of the current shortage of medical doctors was created by decisions to hold back the growth of medical schools over the past two decades.

Universities find it very difficult to shift resources because of the long-term commitment to full-time faculty positions. As they struggle with an ossified version of supply meeting demand, they are essentially aligning themselves with the interests and preferences of young Canadians. This is an acceptable choice if everyone understands that's what's happening and if we all agree young adults are best able to determine how the country should spend its money.

It's a much less acceptable choice if governments, the general public, and employers expect something different. When there's a general belief that universities exist to serve the broader interests of society, as well as the personal academic and career interests of students, the current practice runs off the rails. A few countries direct students towards specific fields and engage in social engineering to produce the "right" number of graduates in the "right" fields. Canada is far removed from this approach and seems content with leaving the shape of the nation's universities largely in the hands of eighteen-year-olds.

Aboriginal Students Put Their Communities First

The change in Aboriginal participation in the Canadian university system has been extraordinary. In the late 1960s only a couple of hundred Aboriginal students attended university. There are now more than 30,000 Aboriginal students in Canada's colleges and universities. And—common assumptions aside—they do not all receive massive subsidies and grants to attend university, even though the Government of Canada has made commitments to expanding financial support for them.

There are some important trends associated with Aboriginal participation. The overwhelming majority of Aboriginal students are female—as much as 85 per cent in some regions—and many of them are single parents. Success rates are not very high, largely because of the gap between the academic standards of predominantly Aboriginal schools and the urban upper-middle-class schools that produce most university students.

Aboriginal students tend to cluster in programs with special support programs, particularly in education and social work, but with expanding numbers in law, administration, nursing, and business. Few special efforts are made to produce Aboriginal historians, biologists, or philosophers, although there are an increasing number of all of these. The Aboriginal graduates are impressive, determined, and dedicated students, often overcoming enormous personal, family, and community challenges to complete their education.

But by far the greatest difference between Aboriginal and non-Aboriginal students is that Aboriginal people put their communities ahead of their own ambition and opportunity. There is a remarkably common question that Aboriginal students ask, in one form or another, of professors, counsellors, and others: how can I best use my education to benefit my community? It's not a question you'll often hear from a non-Aboriginal student.

The reasons for, and the effect of, this desire to put the community first are quite simple. Young Aboriginal people know how badly their communities and organizations need trained and skilled people. Their parents, teachers, community members and—particularly—elders often push talented young people hard to succeed at school and go on to university. What's more, Aboriginal people often place a much higher value on community than the highly individualistic non-Aboriginal student population.

This is why Aboriginal students are more likely to pursue careers of direct benefit to their communities, often broadly defined, and why they are much more likely to see their talents and abilities as a collective resource. It also means that Aboriginal students carry the burdens of their family and community into their studies and often see failure not in personal terms, but rather as though they have let down their community.

There's a remarkable success story in the Aboriginal experience at university. There are now thousands of graduates across the country, moving into various private and public sector positions and enriching and empowering both their communities and the nation. There are now many Aboriginal professional associations—the country is long since past the point where an indigenous PhD, doctor, teacher, lawyer, nurse, or business owner is a rarity. The impact of Aboriginal teacher-education programs alone has had a tremendous impact on Aboriginal education in Canada. And there is now a higher percentage of Aboriginal people with law degrees than the percentage of lawyers for the whole population.

The situation is not all rosy, however. Many of the people who leave remote reserve communities to attend university do not go back. This is particularly true for Aboriginal women, who often remain in the cities and large towns and often marry a non-Aboriginal. Even so, the Aboriginal graduates see their accomplishments and their obligations in very different terms than other university students, who routinely place their career and personal interests well in front of doing what's best for their community or their country.

Cheating and the Internet

Cheating is as old as education, and no doubt began when the first teacher tested the first student. Plato's students probably brought notes into his exams scratched on pieces of pottery. They might have hired an older student to sit their exams, or paid some poor scribe a few drachmas to write their essay. But the days of cheat notes on *ostraka* are long gone. Now students have discovered a whole new world of cheating, with the Internet.

The Internet has proved a powerful tool for illegal academic behaviour. It was bad enough when desktop computers began to provide access to vast amounts of information and "cutting and pasting" was transformed from a kindergarten activity into an essay-building process. Then intellectual criminals—no need to mince words here—created websites where students could buy and download entire essays. Some sites allowed students to specify the grade they wanted: an A, B, or C. No need to draw attention by having a C+ student submit an A+ paper. Writers can earn substantial incomes producing individually written papers for lazy and dishonest students.

Universities are smart places so they quickly found a response. A web service called turnitin.com found its niche in electronically surveying essays for universities to check for plagiarism. It compared this year's papers to ones from earlier years, and to essays handed in at other universities. Students, when caught, are given a small penalty, usually a failing grade on the course (but rarely a permanent mark on the transcript, thus removing a crucial piece of information for potential employers).

Their explanations are usually lame: too much academic work (university's fault), have to work to afford school (parents' fault), didn't know plagiarism was wrong (society's fault), need high grades to get into law school or medicine or to get professional accreditation in engineering or accountancy (the system's fault), paying high sums as an international student and struggling not to disappoint parents (globalization's fault), and on and on.

The problem now extends well beyond copying essays. With the newer technologies, particularly Internet-enabled mobile phones, students can bring the entire textbook—and a thousand other texts for that matter—into an exam setting. Universities can and do fight back. Mobile devices are banned from examination rooms. Signals can be jammed. But with the stakes high and the demand growing, student and criminal ingenuity will continue the process of innovation in academic dishonesty.

There is one good piece of news in all of this. There aren't many crooked students. The vast majority are honest and sincere. They do their homework properly, don't cheat on tests, and use assignments and examinations as learning opportunities. So far at least, the cheaters have not taken over the academy. But it's certainly demoralizing that even a small number have been caught.

What's more important is that cheating (especially when widespread in a particular class or program) undermines the very purpose of the academic enterprise. So far there have been no public scandals about academic integrity. Universities keep these cases quiet where they can. Some day soon, though, a big scandal may break out and, potentially, tarnish the public reputation of the academy.

There's good reason to anticipate that the problem will get worse. The Internet has also transformed thousands of young people—maybe most of them—into petty thieves. The young steal constantly. They rip off music and damage an entire industry. They download movies—most are available on-line the day they enter the theatres—and wreak havoc with the intellectual property of newspapers, publishers, composers, artists, and filmmakers. Check a young adult's iPod, BlackBerry, computer, or other device and you might well find hundreds of dollars worth of stolen content. Parents who would be devastated if their children stole a chocolate bar from the local convenience store think nothing of their kids scouring the web for the latest film and downloading it onto their computer.

The Internet has damaged one of the core moral and commercial principles of our society: that creators own their intellectual property. Young people are remarkably casual about stealing and using what is not theirs. It's not a huge step from downloading movies without paying for them to grabbing an essay or other content off the web and submitting it as one's own. Given that very little is being done to prevent young people from committing this kind of intellectual crime, it is not hard to imagine that the Internet will continue to undermine intellectual integrity, promote dishonesty, and blur the line between original and borrowed ideas.

Students Are Unwilling to Study Abroad

Only 3 per cent of Canadian university students study abroad during their undergraduate years. That's amazing, given that Canadian institutions have dozens of exchange agreements with foreign universities. Our universities offer travel study courses. Queen's University even has a castle in England. Other universities have field stations and campuses in exotic locations. There are hundreds of scholarships and bursaries for international experiences and work placement overseas for adventurous students.

Universities want their students to travel and learn abroad. Professors know the many benefits that come from living overseas. Language and culture programs in particular want students to spend time in a linguistically rich educational environment. French students can go to France (or Quebec if they cannot afford overseas travel), German students to Germany, Asian studies students to Japan, China, or Korea.

There are dozens of signs on every campus promoting travel study classes, exchange agreements, and international bursaries. International offices host information nights and promote overseas experiences. Professors talk up opportunities in class. Many faculty members volunteer to lead students abroad. But few students want to go.

Why is it so? Students in Europe—helped by well-funded European Union exchange agreements—move about regularly. So do Aussies and Kiwis. But Canadians, exposed in schools and communities to people from around the world, just don't seem keen to travel. Maybe they think that visiting the

Asian community of Richmond, BC, the Ukrainian-Canadians of Dauphin, Manitoba, or Little Italy in Toronto is a substitute for the real thing.

Money is a big factor. International travel can be expensive. Highly motivated students find the cash and make the sacrifices necessary to participate. And there are substantial and helpful bursaries available at most universities. Many of the exchange agreements have students pay their fees and room and board at their home universities. The incremental cost is limited to travel expenses (and enough money to pay for local experiences). Governments are getting on the bandwagon. Ontario, in particular, is keen to promote study abroad.

Language used to be a barrier. Unlike European young adults, who are comfortable in several languages, most Canadian students, like their American counterparts, want only English language instruction. But many universities now offer English language courses abroad, often taught by native English speakers and patterned on standard North American courses. It's not a genuine cultural experience, but it's a start, and it removes a major disincentive to overseas study.

The main resistance to studying abroad is cultural. Despite Canada's ethnic diversity, this is a parochial country. Young adults, in the main, are neither worldly nor adventurous. They stick close to home. Even students born and raised abroad appear to limit their travel to return visits to the home country. Canadian youth lack the wanderlust of Scandinavian, Australian, and New Zealand youth. Those who do study abroad tend to cluster by native tongue, limiting contact with local people. In terms of cultural learning, the best thing that can happen is for a Canadian student to get a local boyfriend or girlfriend.

In the globalized, internationally connected world, overseas experience has become a prerequisite for national success. The country needs young people who know Japan, Korea, China, India, the Middle East, Brazil, and other countries and areas well, who speak the language, and who understand local cultures and political environments. The ethnic diversity within Canada needs to be matched by solid connections to the rest of the world.

Universities have to lead this push and urge students to explore distant lands, learn new languages, experience other cultures, and become citizens of the world. To date, Canada and its universities are not doing very well.

Residence Life

A month before the University of Northern British Columbia opened in September 1994 the university learned that the furniture for the residences, including the beds, would not arrive on time. With students arriving in a few weeks, the university hastily made alternate arrangements with city hotels. About 400 brand new students started their careers in temporary quarters, taking buses to and from the campus. When the beds (but not the tables and chairs) arrived, the university shut down the hotel option and the students camped out in their residence rooms. They were not happy, but eventually order was restored. Not an ideal situation, but one that bonded the first-year students and created one of UNBC's first folk memories.

Residences are not simply an "ancillary service" designed to assist students with housing needs. They are an integral part of the academic experience, crucial to student success, and fundamentally important to the nature and vitality of campus life.

First impressions count, and so do first-year experiences. Many students arrive at university full of nervous energy. Away from their parents, among strangers, in a new environment, they experience a combination of liberty and rules, control and freedom. Residences, largely through residence dons (advisors) and residence life programs, monitor the young people, control (most) excesses, and otherwise help students survive and thrive in a strange land.

Residences do more than any other part of the university to tie students to a campus. They provide shared experiences—social occasions, personal oversight, gentle direction—and common disgust with residence food has bound generations of students together. Countless friendships, hookups, and romances find their origins in residence cafeterias, dorms, games rooms, and residence events. Residences ease students from parental control into adulthood and they do so in an arms-length and often very dynamic fashion.

Many students never experience residence life and they are often the poorer for it. Those who commute to campus typically stay with their parents, remain connected to familiar friends and activities, and are pulled away from full engagement in the campus. For them, university attendance lingers for several years as an extension of high school. At the other extreme, students attending universities where most students live in residence— Acadia, Mount Alison, St. Francis Xavier, Bishop's—where the institution dwarfs and defines the host community, have intense experiences that shape their adulthood.

The more in-tune universities understand that residence life is interconnected with academic development. Living-learning communities knit them together nicely. Lectures, seminars, study sessions, and help centres in the residences enrich both the community and the students' academic experience.

Most Canadian universities lag well behind American schools in the development of residence life. Private schools in the states compete for students more with hot tubs and climbing walls than with faculty publications and remedial writing seminars. The elite private institutions offer residence-life arrangements that seem more like academic resorts than university housing. Food courts, however, demonstrate how much has changed. Largely gone are the lineups for the daily dose of mac and cheese or meat loaf, or as at Western in the 1960s, the "dreaded veal cutlet." In their place are multi-island, customer-driven food emporiums. Mom's cooking quickly recedes into memory, replaced by a culinary cornucopia, particularly if you share the food preferences of eighteen-year-old males. *Bon appétit!*

VI
A Professor's Life

Teaching in the Dark Ages

The University of Virginia in Charlottesville, founded in 1800, has a beautiful campus. The centrepiece is a wonderful lecture hall designed by Thomas Jefferson, the founder. The classroom is in the round—the lecturer stands in the middle, with the students arrayed in several tiers above. He talks, they listen. The setting is stunning. You can almost hear two hundred years of lectures and discussion reverberating in the air.

If Thomas Jefferson walked onto a Canadian campus today he'd find that little has changed. Professors stand in front of classes, much larger now, lecturing from a podium. Some classes, and most graduate courses, are offered as seminars, with the instructor the focus of attention. The method of conveying information—and of inspiring students to think great thoughts—hasn't changed much since the early nineteenth century.

There have been some adjustments to new technology. Chalkboards have been replaced with white boards—but the method is the same: handwritten scrawls. Overhead projectors have been superseded by PowerPoint—easier to read, but much the same. A few instructors use clickers—allowing students to respond electronically to instructor's questions—to encourage class participation. More technologically savvy professors have shifted to "mixed modal" instruction, combining lectures and seminars with Internet-based course management and delivery systems.

Students are moving faster than the instructors. They show up to class with portable computers, cell phones, and other gadgets. They are as likely to be sending e-mail or playing a video game as working on class material. Only a very small number of professors ban such devices from the classroom.

What we have in Canada now is a very traditional university system with some small adjustments to accommodate new technologies. The students want—even demand—more. Some want lecture material on-line, making class attendance optional. Many universities have on-line course management systems that centralize grading, assignment submission, and even discussion groups. Many on-campus students sign up for distance-education courses and do them from their residence rooms. At some institutions, 80 per cent or more of the so-called distance registrants are on campus and otherwise attending regular classes.

Canadian universities are facing a revolution in the technological tools available for teaching, but efforts to adapt are few, and rely more on the actions of individual professors than on institutional decisions. Acadia led the way with the "Acadia Advantage," that saw every student receive a portable computer and an attempt to integrate technology campus-wide. Most campuses dabble in new technologies. Business and medical schools are often well equipped with the latest gadgets; the core faculties have to be content with technology-enabled classrooms.

In the United States, where institutions scramble for competitive advantage, and where elite schools have both a lot of money and effective corporate tie-ins, we see many more attempts to capitalize on new technologies. Each new innovation—portable computers, Internet-enabled cell phones, iPods, iPhones, and iPads—has had several campuses leaping to the technological forefront. Canadian schools are much more reluctant to do this, partly because our non-competitive environment does not really reward innovation of this type.

In 1994, as the University of Northern British Columbia was being opened, vendors from across North America descended on the campus. Careful attention was given to many cutting-edge technologies. The list was impressive: the Apple Newton (a precursor of the iPhone, dropped as bad technology), the paperless campus (a Green fantasy), a centralized audio-visual system (a limited success), the one-card system for all on-campus purchases (this one worked), and a unified student information system (avoided in favour of a purpose-built registrarial system that balked at the workload). Most of these—save for the paperless office—are now common-place. Back then, most represented major campus experiments.

So here is the tech conundrum. Universities adopt new technologies slowly and cautiously. Faculty members—who bear the greatest burden for adjusting to new systems—tend to want to teach in much the same way they were taught themselves. Students, in contrast, inhabit the North American version of the technology frontier and want instant adoption of the latest gadgets. Tech-education is in its infancy, believe it or not. Major changes loom: for one thing the days of the traditional lecture may be numbered. But universities are unlikely to be among the first to move.

58 Teaching as Torture

A visiting speaker from Japan, giving an excellent lecture on the continuing importance of industrial activity in the new economy, looked out at a sea of vacant stares and clearly uninterested students. At the end of the talk he said sadly, "It was like hitting golf balls into a fog. You cannot see anything land!"

A few years later, a professor was readying himself for the last lecture of the semester. It was also the day course assignments were due, and they had to be handed in during class time. Five minutes before class time only thirty of ninety students were in the lecture hall. In the last few minutes most of the rest arrived, walked to the front of the class, put their papers on the table by the podium—and left the room. One student arrived five minutes late, walked down the stairs to the front of the class right up to the professor (who was lecturing by that time), dropped the assignment and then double-timed it up the stairs and out of the classroom. Fewer than one-third of the students stayed for the lecture itself.

Some students may be surprised to learn that professors have feelings too. While a handful of profs put their class materials together hastily, most spend hours assembling lecture notes, readings, in-class exercises, and assignments. One colleague, lecturing in English, which is not her native language, estimates she spends ten to twelve hours preparing for each fifty-minute lecture—though hers is an extreme example. When students fail to show up for class, only play computer games, write e-mails during the lecture, or otherwise reveal their profound boredom, professors are understandably distressed.

Superstar professors—every campus has them—rarely have these problems. These exceptional teachers, gifted performers and wonderful communicators, are engaging, funny, emotional, and powerful. Their classes can be tours de force, remembered by students for years. Other brilliant teachers are more low-key, better known for their attention to student needs, their careful handling of course materials, and the careful construction and management of the class.

But many intelligent, reasonably competent, and likable teachers fail to make the top grade. And it is in their classes that the full impact of student disengagement is felt. These earnest and dedicated professors feel the pain of student uninterest—and worry about year-end teaching evaluations.

The front of the classroom can be a lonely place, where isolation grows with the size of the class. Professors are expected to entertain and inform, challenge and comfort, educate and inspire. If there is little feedback—and particularly if the students offer up blank stares, shuffling papers, eating, and other impolite distractions—time at the podium can be torture.

Some of our colleagues, including top-notch professors, suffer through their teaching. One used to throw up before almost every class. Another had a camp cot in his office on which he napped to recover after each lecture. Performing in a classroom takes a great deal out of a person. Just as a dynamic class can be energizing and exciting, an uninspiring class can be truly upsetting.

All professors want much the same thing. They want to educate. They want students to "get" the core information and ideas that form the foundation for future studies. Except for the weird ones—and there are a number of these—they care what the students think of them. They want their students to pursue additional courses in the field. More than anything, they want their students to take insights, ideas, theories, and concepts from the class and carry them out into the world and throughout their lives. Professors love their subject—they devote their lives to it—and are generally very excited about the course content.

Many classrooms, then, are the educational equivalent of giving a carefully chosen gift to a friend—and then to have her lose it, ignore it, or return it to the store for a refund. How demoralizing. Bored, disengaged, and disinterested students suck the intellectual vitality out of a classroom. They rob a wonderful opportunity of its potential and leave it dead on arrival.

59 Universities Should Be Exciting

Slagging universities—they are such easy targets—has long been a blood sport for students, faculty, government officials, employers, and the general public. The lofty ideals of the academic—perfect wisdom, cultural understanding, grand ideas, transformative research, public service, and the careful nurturing of young talent—make it inevitable that universities will fall short of their self-defined mark. Like all human institutions universities have quirks, flaws, odd-duck personalities, and strange systems and procedures that the public finds mystifying.

Leave that aside for a minute. We think that universities are fine places.

They have a great deal to offer: the mixing of ideas, genuinely smart and interesting people, talented and eager students, facilities designed to support the generation of new knowledge, libraries filled with millions of remarkable books and journals, and time to think, talk, listen, learn, and contemplate. But put aside all the practical talk and the preoccupations with career, employment, and practicality, and focus for a moment on the essence of a university—the classroom experience.

First, a basic point. There is no ideal professor, no single teaching style, no essential pedagogical model. Some students respond well to the lovable old prof, the embodiment of traditional academia, with his bow tie, rhetorical phrases, endless fountain of detail, and fondness for classical learning. Others find inspiration with a newly minted female professor, well versed in post-modernist and post-colonial thought, and devoted to engaged in-class debate. The professor who attacks students' prose with the ferocity of a mother bear guarding its cubs can be hated by half the class and loved by the rest. There are professors who, in private conversation, seem boring beyond belief, but who generate real energy and life-long affection from their students. And yes, there are awful ones too.

The university experience is like a visit to the optometrist. You sit down in the chair and the doctor swings a large machine in front of your face. She starts to manipulate the lens. Each time she asks, "Is that clearer? Less clear?" On she goes, narrowing the range of options until a proper prescription is identified for you. No two people are the same—each one has to be tested and challenged independently to identify the right combination of lenses. When students arrive at university, they think they have part of the prescription figured out—arts over engineering, or chemistry over social work. They launch into their first courses. For some the world becomes clearer. For others the lectures make things more opaque. Like the optometrist who is trying to help her patients see well, universities are trying to help students figure out how best to understand the world.

Some students find it impossible to comprehend humanity without a solid grounding in history. Others find that literature, gerontology, psychology, or business best describe and define the world they see and the world they wish to engage with. Those with a broad view of humanity know that language and the culture it reveals are the essence of an education. Still others head to physics (any discipline that can explain the curveball and improve our understanding of curling must be the fount of all important knowledge), chemistry, or biology. Another group, practical problem-solvers by nature, find themselves in engineering. Those seeking to express their creativity might go to architecture or fine arts.

Universities are not about prescribed pathways—although foundational knowledge is essential for an educated and engaged citizen. Universities are about intellectual and social matchmaking. The classes and programs exist to provide students—the young people who will drive any society into the future—with an opportunity to explore their reality and to determine how best to understand the human, natural, and physical world. Students can flounder. Students routinely shift programs and faculties. Engineering students graduate with a degree in sociology. French scholars end up with a Bachelor of Computer Science. Students come to university with imperfect vision—the role of the institution and the professors is to help each one find the best way to see clearly.

This is why universities and university classes are so truly exciting. Watching young people connect with ideas is one of the most remarkable experiences around. A lecture on the history of American slavery makes students confront the reality of racism; a biology class on the potential of nanotechnology opens their eyes to new realities; and an environmental studies course brings the significance of climate change into sharp focus. Intellectual collisions like these, and many others, happen every day at university (though alas, not to every student). Young people discover their world and their place within it. Faculty members challenge students, enlighten them, debate with their classes, and learn, too, from the experience.

Universities can be the most exciting and dynamic places on earth. They show that ideas matter—and that the work of questioning, researching, analyzing, debating, and contemplating the human and natural worlds is far from done. Universities are about uncertainty and about discovery. To be in the classroom—with the students and among the faculty—is a privilege of the highest order. Universities have their faults, for sure, but never forget that they are, first and foremost, the places where young people learn to see. The gift of vision and the ability to question represent the true mission of the university. May it ever be so.

60 It's Hard to Get a Faculty Job

Professors have the best jobs around. The salaries are good, working conditions are superb, and flexibility is first rate. Perhaps this is why they are among the hardest jobs to get in the country.

Think about what it takes to win the faculty job lottery. Start with a four-year undergraduate degree. Get high grades and perhaps a load of debt. Be one of the handful of students accepted to a first-rate Master's program. Ace the courses while applying for scholarships to pay the bills, and/or spend ten hours a week leading tutorials and grading papers. Cultivate professors for letters of reference for a PhD program at one of the top schools.

You got into Prestige University! Now your classmates are all as smart as you, and some are smarter. Keep studying—and never stop applying for grants. Struggle to make a name for yourself in the discipline by giving a few conference papers. If you are lucky your supervisor will help you publish an essay in a good journal. Work on your dissertation. Teach a course or two—you have to learn how sometime, and this is the place to do it. Three or four years pass. Graduate with your PhD.

Now you have a ticket to the big show, but you're not there yet. The universities have given out more tickets than there are seats in the professoriate. There are other jobs—in colleges, with government, and in the private sector—but by now you've been aiming for the big prize for ten years or more. Your professors tell you that you're one of the best. So you persist. You might apply for a post-doctoral fellowship, which will give you a year or two of research time and an opportunity to boost your publication list. But you are only putting off the inevitable job search.

You apply for jobs across the country (your own institution is probably off limits—universities aren't keen on hiring their own). There are a shockingly small number of places to approach. There was so much talk about retiring profs and a hiring boom that you figured you could pick and choose. Now, you just want something to apply for. Few of the jobs match your qualifications precisely, but a little fudging on the application letter doesn't hurt. You coordinate a mass letter-writing campaign in your support. If you're lucky, you'll make a shortlist at an acceptable university. For most, any invitation for a job interview will do.

Many of your friends will end up as "sessionals," teaching on limited term contracts for $35,000 a year. Some will only get a course or two and struggle to live on $15,000. They may do this for years, teaching courses for peanuts, few benefits, and no job security, until they get discouraged and quit.

But you are lucky—you get interviewed for a full-time job. The interviews are tough—a lecture to students, a presentation on your research, a tense meeting with potential colleagues, and a series of meals with members of the search committee. Then a long wait for a call from the Department Chair.

What are the odds you'll make it through? It's hard to be precise. In a few specialized fields—economics, electrical engineering, pharmacy, and accountancy—the success rate approaches 100 per cent. In most others, there are dozens of qualified applicants for every job on offer. In some fields—history, biology, philosophy, and physics—there can be several *hundred* top-notch candidates for a single post.

So you made it to a full-time, tenure-stream position at a Canadian university. Well done. You have landed in clover, caught the brass ring, won the lottery. True, you may be in your mid-thirties by this time, but compulsory retirement has been abolished, so enjoy it as long as your health holds out. Of course, you have to get tenure, and that can be scary, but almost everyone sails over this hurdle without difficulty. Welcome to the good life!

Your Prof Doesn't Take the Summer Off

One thing academics hate to hear the most is this: "It must be nice not to have to work for four months every summer!" Oh that it were so. It's true that profs don't teach in the summer (unless they are young and desperate for money), but almost all of them work surprisingly hard pretty much all year round.

It wasn't always that way. A couple of generations ago many university teachers did spend summers at the cottage, sometimes writing and thinking, but quite often just fishing. The majority never published a book or a major scientific paper—more than a few never published anything. But they were also badly paid, and had some moral right to take long holidays. Very few people do this any more: it would be a career-killer.

The formal workload of a university professor seems pretty easy. A full-time lecturer at a Canadian university will teach two semesters of thirteen weeks each. In the social sciences and humanities a standard teaching load involves three courses a week, three hours in the classroom for each. Scientists often supervise labs. Each hour of class time involves a certain amount of preparation and grading (more or less, depending on the availability of teaching assistants). So each course might involve eight hours of teaching time a week, for a maximum of twenty-four hours.

Many faculty members, though, teach two courses in one semester and three in the next, instead of the standard three and three, and big names can teach even less. But supervision of graduate students, if they have them, can be a huge drain on time. Faculty are also contractually required to do "service" to the university, which mostly means committee work, and since universities are largely self-governing, there is always a lot of this. Then there is the obligation to do research and scholarly publication.

Summer is the time when faculty members are supposed to conduct research, and most of them do, both because they like doing it and because promotion and salary raises largely depend on it. Scholarly work involves conducting research, attending conferences, writing up research results, grant proposals, articles and books, dealing with publishers, and so on.

It's a great life, so long as you value freedom more than money. There are two wonderful things about it. First, once a prof has tenure she is immune to hassles from above, so long as she fulfills her contractual obligations. Despite the alarms raised by faculty unions, the number of academics who have been fired in Canada for dereliction of duty over the past fifty years can probably be counted on the fingers of both hands (though some may have left when shown the writing on the wall). Second is flexibility. Profs can go to work late in the morning so long as they meet their classes, and they can head home early. They can work at home and can adjust their work schedule to accommodate family holidays. They can go to conferences in exotic places. As for research itself, either in a lab or an archives, it doesn't look that onerous to someone who sells real estate for a living.

Some faculty members whine about overwork, and a few waste time in university politics. But most realize how lucky they are to be doing what they love in an atmosphere relatively free of stress. In some ways it's the best job in the world: state funded (and therefore very secure), reasonably well-paid, with tons of flexibility, a great deal of self-direction, and a chance to make a difference—academic or practical—in the world. The overwhelming majority of the faculty realize this. They work hard with their students, on their classes, and on their research.

They are big users of e-mail and stay in touch with professional colleagues around the world. Laboratory scientists are always on call and check in on their equipment regularly. Many contribute to social organizations, consult with governments, advise First Nations agencies, speak to community groups, write op-ed pieces, provide important context and background on the news, and otherwise contribute to making the city, region, and country better.

So professors don't take the summer off. Many work sixty to seventy hours a week and do so without much complaint. Professors work in a thousand different ways, and the overwhelming majority make real and sustained contributions. Just because they are not in their offices, and even though they are home at 3:30 p.m. to collect their kids from elementary school, they are still giving full value for their money.

Tenure Terror

Congratulations, newbie! You now work full time at a Canadian university. But your job is not yet secure. Looming ahead is the most stressful ritual of the academic profession: tenure.

The ability to speak openly about all manner of issues, comfortable or controversial, is the essence of a university. But fifty years ago, university professors did not have total freedom to profess. Those who offended the authorities—by criticizing church doctrine, speaking out on racial or cultural issues, or complaining about the administration of the university—could lose their jobs. Once in a while a prof with left-wing sympathies (alleged or actual) was fired, blacklisted, and otherwise mistreated.

Firings of university professors were not very common in Canada, but the possibility of dismissal cast a chill over the academy. So, how does a university protect faculty members while ensuring the quality and competence of the professoriate? The answer is tenure.

As you start out in your academic career you still have two significant hurdles to climb. First, there is a probationary review. Didn't we tell you? That first permanent contract was not permanent. You have to be reappointed to a second probationary term. If your teaching is not up to standard, if you are not fitting in well with colleagues, or if your research is weak the university can let you go at this stage. The option is rarely used, but it is a real and legal stage in the process.

As your fifth year is ending, you start preparing for the tenure application. This involves a statement about your research, teaching, and service activities; a departmental report on your contributions; and the selection of academic experts at other universities who can comment on your career. Your department will then review your file, sending its recommendations to a faculty-wide committee that makes a recommendation to a university committee, and then the president for a final decision. It's cumbersome, but that's the way universities work.

If the final decision is unfavourable you are out. Most universities give you a last year of employment to sort out your affairs, but tenure denial means the loss of a job. You can try to find another one, but you are marked as a loser. Get turned down for tenure at one school and you could be out of the field forever. Pass the tenure bar and you are in for life. This is one big decision!

Tenure terror describes the long and stressful process leading up to the fateful decision. Junior faculty struggle to make sure they have met qualifications that are never entirely clear. Publish enough papers—but how much is enough? Get enough research grants—but how many? Teach well. Be a good colleague. Show potential. Make a difference professionally. And in the tenure year, sit on pins and needles while department, faculty, and university committees sit in judgment as you wait for the puff of white smoke that means you have passed the second greatest hurdle in your career (the first being to get the job in the first place). If the decision is negative you can appeal through your faculty association/union, but winning tenure this way will leave a nasty taste in your mouth for decades.

The good news for profs is that very few Canadian academics are denied tenure. It's different in the United States, where a substantial percentage of applicants are turned down at the leading universities. At Harvard tenure review is a well-known blood sport with the bar set almost unreachably high—you've published two books, but are they *seminal* books? Happily for you, Canadian schools do not have such ridiculously high standards.

Canadians, after all, are nice folks. Here faculty members in difficulty are often eased out of their positions before the tenure process starts. Frank conversations with department chairs or deans warn that you may get turned down. Many take the hint and seek employment at another institution or a career outside the academy.

Tenure terror is very real. Junior faculty members, even first-rate ones, feel this fear. Knowing that your career hinges on a single decision, made behind closed doors by colleagues in your department and faculty, is nerve-racking in the extreme. If the vote is negative you are crushed. If it's positive, lucky you. You're virtually unfireable.

Universities Don't Evaluate Professors Properly

Universities are intensely competitive environments. Students compete for grades and scholarships. Graduates compete for places in graduate school. Faculty members compete for research grants and academic prestige; they compete for tenure and promotion, and often for an annual merit bonus; and they work in a complex professional environment, where evaluation is constant, real approval rare, and criticism routine and intense.

Given all of this, it's not surprising that universities have worked out well-understood methods of evaluation. The currency of academic life is well known: publications in refereed scholarly journals (reviewed by anonymous colleagues in the discipline) and university presses count first. Some disciplines even have elaborate statistical processes for figuring out the "impact" of a specific article. Securing a competitive research grant is highly rated, as are invited lectures—particularly those at prestigious universities. Effective teaching is taken seriously, but not as much as academic publications. Other things—patents, conference papers, contract research, university research, and service to the university or the profession—also count, but not as heavily as the journal articles and academic books.

But just look at what's not on the list. Presenting academic knowledge to the general public or to special interest groups is not generally accorded high value. Writing opinion pieces in the newspaper is seen as unimportant, even frivolous. Documentary film production is seen as a lesser achievement. Being quoted regularly in the media is often frowned upon as being unserious. Assisting community groups with program design or evaluation attracts little attention and few rewards. And working with a company on new product development is not seen as prime scholarly work.

In short, work targeted at the scholarly community is accorded the highest value. Contributions of a more general nature, and not subject to peer review, are weighted much less heavily.

The system needs to change—not to eliminate the importance of academic contributions but rather to recognize the value of contributions to the community at large. There's no single model for academic performance, and it's not appropriate that the definition of professional work be a narrow one. Some academics will focus their entire working lives on scholarly articles and books. This is perfectly fine and should be encouraged and—when there is high-level accomplishment—recognized and rewarded. But with a fairer system for evaluating faculty, most scholars would likely end up balancing academic and other contributions, serving both the scholarly and the non-academic communities. A very small number of university professors would choose, if the reward system permitted it, to focus their efforts on community outreach and knowledge mobilization. They should be recognized for this effort and rewarded appropriately.

University professors are like other professionals. They respond to incentives—a high salary, promotion, status, recognition, and prestige—and they shape their professional lives accordingly. Early in their career, as they seek tenure and promotion, they generally work for approval from their academic peers and focus their efforts on scholarly activities. Breaking out of this pattern later in their careers can be difficult. By changing the reward and recognition system to include contributions off-campus and to the community at large, universities would send a crucial signal to new and other faculty members. Broadening the list of activities that the institutions endorse through their reward systems would go a long way towards encouraging greater academic-community interaction and would help break down barriers between university researchers and the public at large.

 ## Your Professor Is Not Overpaid

Each year the province of Ontario releases a list of everyone employed by government-funded agencies who earns more than $100,000 a year. The list generates a feeding frenzy as journalists looking for a cheap hit decry the outrageous salaries of civil servants and the malignant growth of the fat-cat bureaucracy. It makes for good blood sport at the expense of civil servants, and who cares about them? Universities are included on the list, and university faculty are among the fastest to scour the list for signs of injustice—does that idiot down the hall really earn $2,000 a year more than I do? The president makes four times my salary! *Aux barricades!*

There's more madness than method in this ritual. The symbolic $100,000 figure was picked several years ago, and has not been adjusted since then. As a result the number of people earning this sum or more has increased dramatically—largely because of negotiated salary increases and standard progression through the ranks. The current figure is roughly comparable to a $70,000 annual salary at the time the annual salary data was started. Ironically, the update encourages salary growth, as people identify themselves as underpaid and use the information to press their employer for more money.

The number of university faculty members making more than $100,000 a year—check out business school salaries if you want your eyes to pop out—naturally raises questions about the size of university pay packets. Most people think university faculty members have a pretty cushy job, with many other benefits not available to most workers. Although this isn't wrong, we think that university professors are not overpaid and that university salaries are very much in line with comparable wages in the Canadian economy.

The high salaries paid to profs in business, law, and medicine are set by international market pressures. Since Canada has one of the best university systems in the world it's hardly surprising that elite universities in the United States, the United Kingdom, and increasingly, East Asia come looking for talent in this country. With these competitors offering well over $200,000 a year for top people in high-demand areas, Canadian schools either have to be competitive or accept mediocrity. Most Canadian schools can't pay top dollar and rely instead on faculty attachment to Canada and the country's quality of living to convince them to take a Canadian job.

Don't forget the investment that faculty members make before they secure a faculty position: an undergraduate degree, usually a Master's degree, a PhD degree, and several years as a low-paid post-doctoral fellow or sessional teacher. And most researchers pay a substantial portion of their research costs and professional activity throughout their careers—a fact that's often ignored. Most faculty do not secure a tenure-stream faculty position until they are in their thirties, a full half-decade later than those seeking regular professional positions.

Finally, we need to put faculty salaries into context. Most high school teachers start around $55,000. In ten years or so they have reached their maximum of $85,000, subject to future pay raises, and they are still in their early thirties. Teachers have much less training than a faculty member with a PhD and typically have spent much less money on their education. The average salary level for university professors is high, but it takes them twenty years to reach the rank of Full Professor. They won't pull level with a high school teacher until they are well into their forties. Faculty should not complain about their salaries—not very many do, off-campus anyway—but they don't need to be overly defensive. University faculty are paid what they are worth. Few give less and many give more than fair value for the money they earn.

65 The Days of Academic Conferences May Be Numbered

The Waikoloa Hotel on Hawaii's Anaeho'omalu Bay seems a strange place to discuss social, economic, and political developments of northern and remote regions, but it's a nice perk for academics with the Western Regional Science Association, escaping their campuses in mid-winter. As you might guess, more than one colleague has found beaches, whales, and orchids far more interesting than multi-paper sessions by earnest academics. Some show up for their sessions, but generally they spend more time with mai tais than lectures. One tried to combine the two and fell off the podium.

This conference was not a total boondoggle. The sessions were superb, and many great ideas were exchanged. Other, more prestigious conferences failed to match this gathering for academic rigour and intellectual value. A recent gathering of 5,000 social scientists in a major American city was notable mainly for the meagre attendance at most sessions. Some panels attracted only a handful of audience members, rendering the whole exercise largely irrelevant. But boondoggle or not, the days of these conferences may be numbered.

Academic conferences are a multi-billion-dollar industry. Almost all scholarly associations have annual meetings. In Canada the Congress of Learned Societies attracts more than 7,000 people to its two-week series of academic meetings. Journalists cruise the Congress looking for papers with silly-sounding topics, candidates for the "Ig Nobel" Prize. Large medical and scientific conferences provide researchers with access to the latest results from the best labs in the world. The key sessions are standing-room-only and produce newsworthy presentations on cutting-edge discoveries.

Other faculty members meet in tiny workshops of a dozen or fewer people to discuss very narrow and esoteric topics. Regardless of size, these meetings allow scholars to get together with researchers with similar interests and for the presentation and debate of the latest research.

So why are academic conferences unlikely to continue in their current form? First, cuts to institutional budgets are reducing faculty travel, so that participants will have to pay part or all of their expenses. Second, at some point university faculty—individually and then collectively—will step up to the climate change plate by refusing to engage in carbon-heavy travel. Declining attendance accelerates very quickly—if fewer scholars attend, the event becomes less interesting to other faculty.

But the real threat is technological. Until now conferences have played a crucial role. Academics love to talk, and they need to talk. Researchers with new discoveries, or exciting interpretations, have to test their ideas with their peers. But new technologies are changing the dynamics entirely. In some disciplines, researchers circulate draft papers electronically, getting feedback that helps them revise the paper. Video streaming, video-conferencing and the rapid decline in the costs of satellite transmission make it much easier to converse without travel. Scholars can reach thousands instead of dozens through podcasts and videoposts distributed through iTunes and other such sites.

In other words, many of the benefits of conferencing no longer need costly travel. Indeed, new technologies greatly expand the reach of new ideas and opportunities for intellectual exchange, especially as the generation raised on iPods, BlackBerrys, instant messaging, and the Internet take over the professoriate.

Conference travel is a real perk for professors, so we can expect ferocious resistance to change. And there are professional development and networking options that are not easily replicated electronically (although this is overstated). But over time scholarly discourse will go digital, and academic conferences will slowly recede, joining illustrated lantern-slide lectures in the recesses of academic memory. It won't be the same as the papaya breakfast at the Waikoloa, though.

66 It's Almost Impossible to Fire Profs

It's not totally impossible, but it's much more difficult than it ought to be. In the past profs usually lost their jobs due to political incorrectness—typically a prof with progressive political leanings running afoul of more conservative administrators. Frank Underhill, the University of Toronto historian was almost fired in 1941 for predicting (correctly) that Canada would drift away from the British Empire and become more American. Harry Crowe did lose his job at United College (now the University of Winnipeg) in 1958 for criticizing the administration, particularly the role of the Presbyterian Church, which still ran the place in those days.

Today the main reason faculty members are fired is not for speaking their minds, but either for gross professional misconduct—the traditional offence is sexual activity with a student—or for flagrant violation of contract, an example being the physics prof at the University of Ottawa who was recently fired because he refused to grade his students, and when the administration insisted, gave them all an A+. A similar example was the prof at the University of Prince Edward Island who was suspended after he offered students a B- to leave his class, which he felt was overcrowded. These people bucked the system, but one thing that profs are never fired for is laziness and incompetence.

At most universities, faculty members are expected to teach, conduct research, and perform "service," usually a combination of committee work and other discipline-related activities inside and outside the university. Some institutions evaluate or review performance only at promotion time, which means that a person promoted to full professor at forty-five could work another twenty years without a further comprehensive review. Other places have annual or bi-annual reviews.

Whatever system is used, though, it's difficult—to the point of impossibility—to fire a seriously underperforming faculty member. The rules make it sound as though this were not true. The Queen's University collective agreement, for example, says that a tenured member may be fired for "gross misconduct, incompetence or persistent neglect of academic duties. Gross misconduct includes a pattern of serious misconduct." All of these terms are subject to interpretation, and of course a faculty member facing termination can appeal, launch grievances, go to the courts, and generally delay the process for years.

The main reason why terrible teachers can't be fired is that many universities have no really sound process in place for assessing them. Incompetence is difficult to prove. How do you prove that a prof is a bad teacher, when the only assessment is an annual form turned in by students answering questions such as "does she seem to have a good grasp of the material?" Good luck going to court with that.

If a faculty member serves on a committee or two, preferably ones that meet only a couple of times a year, goes to a conference once in a while, writes a book review now and then, or co-publishes a scientific paper with twenty other researchers, it's difficult to prove total neglect of duty. Add this to the years of paperwork involved and the hassles with faculty unions, and you can see why most administrators conclude that it's not worth the trouble to get rid of a bad apple or two. In truth, such apples make up only a tiny fraction of faculty members. Perhaps the system that makes it so hard to fire them is the price the universities pay to keep tenure safe. Too bad though, since it's the students and colleagues who suffer.

 ## Faculty Unions

Why on earth do faculty need unions? Far removed from the worlds of Norma Rae, the Wobblies, or the Canadian Auto Workers, faculty members have what the Chinese call an "iron rice bowl"—life-long jobs, career decisions made primarily by colleagues, excellent salaries, tremendous fringe benefits (including funded sabbaticals), a great deal of flexible time, and lovely working conditions. It's hard to imagine there's much left to fight for. The idea of faculty forming a union and going on strike for major improvements must seem ridiculous to most Canadians. More than a few university administrators think the same thing.

But you can make a good argument that they are necessary. Any large group of employees needs and deserves standardized arrangements, with some flexibility based on performance and competitive considerations. Those few places without formal faculty unions have faculty associations that perform almost all the same functions—they just don't have a legal right to strike. Universities cannot deal independently with hundreds of employees; they require structure as much as the faculty members do. There are hundreds of complexities in the work place—from harassment policies to appeals of tenure decisions—that require formal arrangements. Universities could, in the absence of a union/association, impose the rules, but they would pay a high price in terms of confusion, overlap, and faculty unhappiness. Likewise, salary negotiations would be incredibly difficult without the constructive (or occasionally, less than helpful) intervention of faculty representatives.

Faculty associations and unions are enormously helpful in resolving the often-intense personnel matters that arise in an employee-centric environment like a university. The vast majority of troublesome cases are handled through behind the scenes negotiations, and not through formal grievance and appeal procedures. Indeed—and contrary to the popular view of faculty unions—unions and associations are often just as stalwart in the defence of academic quality and professional conduct as the administration. Conflicts typically happen over process—was a decision made in a manner consistent with natural justice and the existing faculty union/association agreement with the university?

Serious conflicts are surprisingly rare at Canadian university campuses. Strikes, which can be as nasty as any workplace confrontation, are noteworthy largely by their absence. Faculty members only go to the wall in exceptional circumstances and when they are extremely angry at the administration. Some of these conflicts have been memorable. In the late 1990s, a Maritime university facing the loss of an entire semester took drastic action. Rather than have the students lose their semester (and the university lose its money), the senior administration offered to set and mark final examinations for all students in all courses—and threatened to lock out the faculty for an additional four months. The faculty caved.

In recent years, most of the harshest conflicts have erupted between the administration and contract teachers and graduate students. The latter two groups feel—with justification—that they are being overworked and underpaid. Expect conflicts of this nature to expand in the coming years, as the teaching burden continues to shift to those without the security of tenure.

Tenured faculty members are treated extremely well—deservedly so—and they need unions or associations to represent their complex and often competing interests. But when they step over the line towards worker solidarity and the rhetoric of labour protest they sometimes find themselves in a different situation than their brothers and sisters on the factory floor and in the mining camp. They may not always elicit sympathy for their cause. The faculty association at a New Zealand university once called its members out on a one-day protest over stalled salary negotiations. Someone had the bright idea to dress up in academic regalia and solicit support along the major routes entering the university. Placard-carrying faculty members decked out in their university finery attracted a vigorous response—people driving by gave them the Kiwi equivalent of the finger. Not exactly the solidarity they had hoped for.

68 The Shame of the Sessionals

The Canadian university system has developed into a class system. At the top of the food chain are the research professors (holding Canada Research Chairs or endowed chairs), who teach very little and can do pretty much what they want with their time. In the middle are the majority of the professors, holders of tenured or tenure-stream faculty positions. At the bottom is an ever-growing army of casual, part-time, contract lecturers—often described as sessionals—who focus on undergraduate teaching and who get neither ongoing support for research nor job security.

Sessionals, hired to fill in gaps in departmental teaching requirements, were originally graduate students. Some had completed their PhDs and were either working on post-doctoral fellowships or in a holding pattern waiting for a full-time position. Some were well-qualified and well-trained individuals who just wanted to work part time. Teaching a course or two did not provide much money, but it helped. For people just entering the profession it was a good way to gain experience and put a couple of notches on their resume. (Some sessionals are experts in a field hired from the community to teach a course: lawyers, accountants, or artists—but these people are generally not teaching out of a dire need for money, and are not the ones we are concerned with here.)

Here's how it works. Professor X is going on a year's sabbatical. The usual arrangement is that she takes a 20 per cent pay cut. She's fairly senior and makes $125,000 a year, so she goes away on a $100,000 salary for that year. She usually teaches four one-semester courses, but only one has to be taught the year she's gone. The university hires a sessional for $6,000 (that's at the low end—at some places they make twice that per course). She gets her leave, a sessional gets hired, and the university saves $19,000. Everyone's happy.

But here is another, more modern scenario. Professor Y is retiring. He also makes $125,000 a year, but teaches five one-semester courses. His university wants all five courses taught. It could hire five sessionals, pay them $6,000 each, and save $95,000. Or it could hire one "full-time sessional" and pay her $35,000 to $50,000, depending on the institution. Often she would teach not five, but six courses for this salary. The higher course load is justified by the fact that the sessional is not expected to do research or sit on committees, just teach.

See how appealing this is to the university administration? The same number of courses are taught, or even more, and they save thousands of dollars. And if you can save that much on one retirement, imagine how much you can save on ten, or thirty. The upshot is that universities increasingly hire sessionals, especially to teach first- and second-year courses, resulting in a two-tiered faculty, where the lucky tenured ones teach a few senior courses for a high salary, and the junior, untenured ones teach lower division courses for a pittance.

The *Socialist Voice* calls them "a flexible, underpaid, university proletariat," which is exactly what they are. They are usually hired on limited-term contracts, often a course at a time or for a single semester or year, so that the university does not become obliged to hire them permanently and does not have to pay benefits. One unnamed Canadian university reported that half its undergraduate English courses were taught by sessionals.

It can be a horrible life for a young academic, teaching a year or two here, another year there, or cobbling together two or three courses at different places—a morning course at Trent in Peterborough, say, and an afternoon course at Toronto's Scarborough campus. In an extreme case, a professor on the prairies taught fifteen separate sections of math in a single year—primarily the first-year math class—at four different institutions. People actually maintain these balancing acts, hoping to get on the tenure ladder, working without pension or other benefits and without access to the research grants needed to make big advances in their academic career.

It's tough to get out of what an official of the Canadian Association of University Teachers calls an "academic ghetto," because people are hired for tenure positions largely on research, and full-time sessionals rarely have the time or money to do much of that. Some people toil in this ghetto for years before getting discouraged and finding another career.

There is another issue here, rather more delicate in nature. Universities brag about the number of tenure-stream faculty members teaching under-graduate classes; *Maclean's* annual university rating issue has made this a marker for commitment to excellence. But do the students care? It's hard to say, but anecdotally students are just as impressed with sessional instructors as they are with full-time professors. There are great and mediocre teachers in each group, the major difference being that poor sessional teachers are rarely invited back. Off they ride into the wilderness in search of another short-term, ill-paid appointment.

It's a bad, exploitive situation, and it's going to get worse. Universities continue to overproduce PhDs in many fields (while underproducing in others, but few history scholars want to switch to finance or electrical engin-eering). A huge infusion of government money would allow universities to staff up, eliminating both the need for so many sessionals and the tiny fingerhold that thousands of sessional faculty have on an academic career. Government funding of that scale is not going to happen, nor are tenured faculty likely to fill the need by teaching more. Increasingly, sessionals themselves have taken action by unionizing. In the meantime, shame on government and the universities for permitting this situation to continue.

The Strange Economics of Scholarly Publishing

Every February Canadian writers, academics among them, look for a special envelope—the annual cheque from the Public Lending Rights Commission. This is a government-funded organization that supports Canadian writers. Every year it polls ten secretly selected libraries. Every time your book appears you get about $30 (it varies year by year). If the book is in all ten libraries you get $300; if you have ten books in ten libraries you get $3,000 (the maximum permitted). Access Copyright, a similar program, provides payments for writing copied for distribution and use. This program pays for use of scholarly journals, among other publications.

For academics, whose royalties from university presses, as we know only too well, would hardly buy a case of beer, and are more often nothing after a year or two, the PLR payment is like manna from heaven. It is also one of the only bright spots in an otherwise dreary scholarly publishing world.

Scholarly publishing is a strange enterprise. Academics don't publish for direct financial benefit—or if they do, they are almost always disappointed. But the indirect returns, in the form of merit pay, outstanding performance bonus, and promotion, can be considerable. If faculty members tell you they don't make any money from publishing, don't believe it! A good publishing year can produce early promotion and a permanent salary increase of $1,000 or more, paid out for the rest of the faculty member's career, factored into pensions. So a book published early in a career could be worth $50,000.

This explains why university teachers are willing to publish in journals that have "page charges"—that is, the author has to pay the publisher so many dollars per page. We've never done it, but it's common in the sciences.

Scholarly journals/magazines typically fall into two groups: journals produced and subsidized by academic associations and those produced by for-profit companies. The latter are particularly important in the scientific and medical fields. In certain areas—neuropsychology but not Canadian history, biochemistry but not English literature—the journals are incredibly expensive and produce substantial profits for their owners. How expensive? A subscription to the journal *Brain* costs close to $1,000 a year. Universities have tried unsuccessfully to break the dominance of the biggest journal publishers, but professors' desire to publish in these prestigious journals has limited the effectiveness of these efforts.

Canadian academic book publishing operates in a similarly odd way. Few trade (for-profit) publishers produce academic books and then usually only from marketable "star" quality academics such as John English, Mark Kingwell, Thomas Homer-Dixon, Frances Westley, and Richard Florida. A small number of university presses produce the vast majority of Canadian scholarly books. Book prices are a real deterrent to the general public and dampen whatever market enthusiasm is left—even for books written in accessible prose.

Academic work focuses on the production and publication of scholarly research. Because of government and university support, the profit motive doesn't enter into the equation. Little effort is devoted to pursuing readership among academics and even less among the general public. The university system produces ever more articles and books, most of which attract very few readers or purchasers. The scholarly writing has much less impact than the system assumes and wants. Many words are printed. Not all are read.

 ## PhDs Don't Drive Taxis

If they do, they are either conducting some sort of research, seeing how the other half lives for a while, or their careers have hit a titanic iceberg. In general though, the taxi driver with the advanced degree is a pretty rare phenomenon. Even someone who has earned a PhD in a field where job prospects are tiny—say, a degree in Classical Greek Literature with a dissertation on Aristophanes' *The Frogs*—will likely not have to take such a stressful, ill-paying job.

The taxi cliché (academics call this a "meme") is really just a stand-in for the idea that there are highly educated people who can't get the jobs they were educated for, and thus, by extension, university degrees are a waste of time and money. There's some truth to this. It can be very difficult for a PhD to get a PhD-level job, but there's a big difference between lowering your sights somewhat and driving a taxi.

In 2001, the average total lifetime income of working Canadians with different levels of education was as follows, though the difference seems to have declined since then:

Grades 9 to 11	$1.07 million
High school diploma	$1.18 million
College diploma	$1.36 million
Bachelor's degree	$2.15 million

It's obvious what a huge advantage having an undergraduate degree makes in many, though not all cases. But it seems that having a PhD does not give a big salary advantage over a Master's. A 2007 survey of Canadians holding graduate degrees, taken two years after graduation, found that while people with Master's degrees earned $60,000, those with doctorates earned only $5,000 more. Considering how much longer it takes to get a PhD, and how much debt graduates sometimes take on, it hardly seems worth the effort, from a financial point of view.

Undergraduate degrees often do pay off in terms of lifetime income. Young people know that, which is a main reason they go to university. For graduate degrees, however, the financial gain is less clear. A PhD gets her first steady job in her thirties, while a high school teacher has been working for ten years and is near the top of the salary ladder. You don't get a PhD to get rich—the rewards are not monetary—but you rarely end up driving a taxi.

VII
Universities in Canadian Society

There's a New Quiet Revolution in Quebec

English-speaking students and professors visiting Quebec in the mid-1970s were often in for a rude shock. The province's university campuses were heavily radicalized, having provided the intellectual direction and passion behind the Quiet Revolution and the rise of the separatist movement. Now they are at it again, but in a very different way. Quebec's universities are playing a key role in the economic transformation and competitiveness of the provincial economy, and have made themselves a force to be reckoned with in the international university landscape.

The new-look Quiet Revolution is markedly different. Gone are the flamboyant speeches, but the fiery nationalism survives. The new revolution is based on the belief that Quebec and the Quebecois can compete economically, and that they can do so without surrendering their souls to English-speaking political parties or companies. The battlefield has shifted, too, from history and political science departments—surprisingly, even disappointingly quiescent in recent years—to the business schools and some of the leading technology centres.

The new Quebec is something to admire. Assertively Quebecois, but comfortably bilingual, French-Canadian students and researchers are much less radicalized than thirty years ago. Many Quebecois students attend English-language institutions, graduates move easily in Canadian and international business environments, and universities play a vital role in regional and provincial development.

Montreal is one of the richest academic-community environments in North America, with a wonderful slate of first-rate institutions: McGill, Université de Montréal, Université de Québec à Montréal, Concordia University, and the under-rated École Polytechnique. Laval University in Quebec City is a fine university, no longer as highly rated internationally as U de M and McGill, but still one of the best humanities and social science universities in North America.

Where Quebec universities really stand out—aided, it must be said, by aggressive provincial government involvement—is in the development of the provincial economy. Montreal has emerged as a Canadian leader in pharmaceuticals and aerospace. Sherbrooke (only recently an industrial dinosaur) has shown great creativity and determination, led by the Université de Sherbrooke. Quebec City, backed by Laval's strong commitment to provincial evolution, is emerging as a creative and high-technology centre. HEC Montreal (formerly the École des Hautes Études commerciales de Montréal) is one of the most impressive and active business schools in Canada, highly regarded internationally and with superb business connections inside the province. The MBA programs at HEC consistently rank among the top in North America and internationally. Almost a third of their students are international—an illustration of how Quebec business programs are leading the province into the global economy.

Quebec's last revolution was very noisy, and the impact of the rise of Quebec separatism still reverberates across the country. This new revolution is subtle and yet equally transformative. Quebec is forging a substantial presence in the national and international marketplace—Lavelin and Bombardier are just the best known of a group of impressive companies.

Provincial universities, the pride of Quebec's post-1960 renaissance, have maintained a crucial role in this latest recasting of the province's place within Canada and the world.

Academic Freedom Is Endangered by Neglect

Academic freedom is guaranteed in Western countries and hasn't been seriously threatened in Canada for fifty years. Why worry about it now?

Faculty members worry about *any* intrusion on their academic freedom. They want, and need, the right to "speak truth to power," to criticize governments, business, and the status quo. They insist on the ability to research controversial topics and to offer radical ideas. This is the essence of the university.

Some academics are concerned about matching funds from business, the possibility of corporate interference, the growing influence of donors in universities, and the concentration of media power in Canada. These are legitimate concerns, and universities have to ensure that ideas—controversial or not—flow freely and openly.

Remember that Canadian academics have spoken powerfully about poverty issues, women's rights, mistreatment of First Nations people, environmental concerns, numerous government policies, homosexuality, and thousands of other controversial topics. Faculty members have a responsibility to interrogate their world and inform the broadest possible constituency about the problems, solutions, and misuses of power.

Conservatives charge that if there is a threat to academic freedom, it lies as much inside the academy as outside, that if any topics are forbidden in universities, it's right, not left-wing ones—pro-, not anti-life; Tom Flanagan, not David Suzuki. There's some truth to this. It's been a long time since any Marxist's job was endangered for political reasons, but extreme right-wing opinions, like those of Philippe Rushton, lead to calls for dismissal. (Rushton, a psychology prof at the University of Western Ontario, had controversial views on race that led David Suzuki to demand he be "rooted out." To its credit, the university refused.) As this is being written, the shameful role of Allan Rock, president of the University of Ottawa, in an attempt to muzzle Ann Coulter, the abrasive American far-righty, has been revealed. In fairness, though, the far-lefty George Galloway was also prevented from speaking (though by the government, not the universities— McMaster and St. Mary's—to which he was invited).

Most debate within universities is fairly moderate, though perhaps because the biggest battles are behind us. The rights of women, First Nations, gays, ethnic minorities, and others—though not fully won—have been substantially addressed, and what used to be voices crying in the wilderness about the environment have become mainstream. But many aspects of contemporary society remain in need of informed and critical commentary.

There must be academic freedom in Canadian universities. Faculty need the right to research what they want, publish what they can, and say what they can defend. But this right carries an obligation to engage, to share ideas, and to risk the criticism that attends controversy. Canadian universities offer strong protection for academic freedom. Canadian academics have not exercised this powerful right and responsibility to the full extent.

There are some Canadian scholars who express controversial views in public—Frances Widdowson (Mount Royal University), Tom Flanagan (Calgary), Anthony Hall (Lethbridge), to cite only Albertan examples. We might disagree with many of their ideas but applaud their willingness to hold unpopular and provocative opinions.

Ironically, when we discussed the writing of this book with colleagues, we were told by more than one that publishing such a book would harm our careers. One even said, "you will never get another academic administrative job in Canada." The idea that an academic would be punished professionally for sharing ideas about the academy is ridiculous (but not *totally* ridiculous). Many of our best academic leaders share with us a passionate belief in the value of universities and a concern about current directions. That we would be warned off writing such a book for fear of professional repercussions is a sad indication that some of the toughest limits on academic freedom are indeed imposed inside the university.

Language Study Is in Decline

Full disclosure: one of us cannot speak another language and has only a scanty reading knowledge of French. The other is more proficient and has enough of several other languages to at least sound erudite. We share a belief, however, in the fundamental importance of language instruction and of gaining the cultural understanding that goes with knowing another language, to say nothing of the economic advantages.

Until fairly recently, proficiency in a second language (almost always French for Anglophones) was a requirement for high school graduation and university admission everywhere in Canada. It still is in many places. Being competent in a language other than English was a key sign of an educated and cultured mind, one of the things that "every educated person should know."

Times have changed. Latin, German, and Greek are all but dead in the public high school system. University course enrolments in these languages are also down sharply across Canada. There is no royal road to mastering another language, and, leaving aside French immersion, fewer students these days are willing to make the necessary effort to do so. Besides, many argue, English has become the global language (four years ago there were 300 million Chinese studying our language), removing the need for Canadian students to expand their studies beyond French. The closure or amalgamation of foreign-language (that is, other than English or French) programs and departments at universities has become depressingly commonplace.

True, plenty of students are studying Asian languages, but the steady growth of these classes, especially Chinese and Japanese, has been dominated by students of Asian ancestry. Students who grew up with Chinese can make a much faster adjustment to Japanese, and vice versa, than students raised speaking only English or French. To make matters worse, it seems that Canadian companies rarely value foreign-language ability and cultural understanding. Graduates of foreign-language programs do not find employers beating a path to their doors. The incentive to learn another language has to be personal more than financial.

The loss, to the students and to Canada, is considerable. Students who learn another language improve their own. Those who don't are missing the cultural insights that accompany mastery of another language. And they lose the capacity to function comfortably in other countries and societies.

Canadians, who constantly boast about our multicultural character, have a limited capacity to speak to each other, let alone to the rest of the world. We pale by comparison to northern Europeans, for example, and share only with the United States the deep cultural myopia of unilingualism. Is it better that 300 million Chinese speak English than a substantial number of Canadians speak Chinese? We don't think so. Sadly, intellectual laziness and cultural blinders mean that the problem of language learning is only going to get worse.

Successful Universities Need a Ton of Money

Governments provide a ton of money to universities. Annual per-student grants, building funds, indirect costs of research payments, and specialized research awards attract lots of attention. But actual government expenditures on universities go far beyond this, and may be 30 to 40 per cent higher than most Canadian realize. Much of this hidden expenditure, surprisingly (or not, for the realist), goes in the form of payments to the upper-middle-class and the wealthiest Canadians. Here's how it works:

Example One: Donors to Canadian universities get tax receipts for their donations. At the most basic level, a cash donation reported on an individual return, donors receive a percentage of their donation back in the form of a tax refund. A $10,000 donation is actually made up of $7,000 in private cash and $3,000 in public funds.

Example Two: Recently the government changed the regulations governing the donations of shares to charities, including universities. Someone who bought shares at $1 and sold them years later for $100 a share would pay capital gains tax on the $99 per share difference. Under the new rules, if an individual donates the shares to a charity, such as a university, she pays no capital gains tax but gets a tax receipt for the full $100 value of the shares. The actual impact depends on an individual's tax situation, but the rules essentially mean that the government is foregoing about 40 per cent in lost taxes. In effect it is allowing the donors to direct those "taxes" to the charity of their choice. This reduces the net cost of the donation to the donors—they get public credit for the full value—and the government is again supporting the university (or other charity).

Example Three: Elsewhere we discuss the manner in which low tuition fees, tuition deductibility (typically by the parents), and tax-protected educational savings plans (with a nice federal grant on top of the personal contribution) represent a major subsidy for wealthy Canadians. They are also subsidies for the university, for they encourage a higher level of university attendance than would be the case if students had to pay a higher percentage of the cost. For the wealthy, these government arrangements can cover half or more of the cost of attending university. For the poor, the impact is negligible.

Example Four: Towns and cities love universities. They lend "class," and are a draw for employers. In return, the municipalities provide some nice financial support, either in the form of property tax free status, contributions equal to all or most of the taxes, or investments in university infrastructure. These arrangements can run into millions of dollars a year, a healthy bonus for the institution.

Example Five: Student loans seem like a fair deal for the taxpayer, for they have repayment plans built into them. But remember two things. First, students pay no interest on the loans until six months after they graduate—another silent subsidy. In 2007, there were just under a million student borrowers, with a total debt to the government of more than $8 billion—a good chunk of it interest-free money. Second, the default rate on loans for university and college students is more than 15 per cent (private college students 25 per cent more than public). Governments surrender millions of dollars to students who default ($70 million as long ago as 1996–97), often to students who failed to complete their studies. For tax-payers, this is another indirect subsidy for colleges and universities.

Successful universities require a great deal of money, and we have no problem with government support for the enterprise. There are major gaps, however, in public knowledge about the extent of government subsidies, tax concessions, and other means of support. People know governments provide a lot of money for universities. Little do they know how much.

Core Courses Are a Good Idea... Or Not

This is the other issue on which the authors have a major disagreement. One of us thinks they are a fine idea, while the other, though not denying this, thinks that given our universities' hunger for students, they simply won't work. We invite the reader to judge our cases.

On the one hand...

Most Canadian universities have abandoned one of their main respon-sibilities. Many of their disciplines refuse to define what a well-educated, properly prepared undergraduate student should study and learn. Contrast two standard faculties: engineering and arts. In the former, and with the help of a vigilant professional association, incoming students are given a rigidly prescribed set of courses. The first year is generally completely fixed, with few if any elective courses. Faculties of arts are dramatically different.

Students rarely have a defined major. Instead, they enter as intellectual free agents, able to sup freely at an academic smorgasbord. No constraints for arts students; they can take whatever they like.

On the surface, the logic of the more open and flexible arrangement is compelling. Imagine telling incoming students, finally freed from the shackles of high school, that they have no choice in what they take. Incoming students do not want paternalistic faculty members telling them what to do. Indeed, why not open the world to them, and let them study whatever they like? Over a short time, the argument goes, they will explore the academic universe, develop an interest, and gain precisely the kind of broad, comprehensive education for which the liberal arts are known.

Unfortunately, the smorgasbord approach to first-year course selection, does not serve a large number of students. Many students—it is impossible to be precise here—do not head off in a great intellectual treasure hunt, testing out new fields of endeavour and exploring new disciplines. Instead, most first-year students appear to follow a safe approach: study things they were good at in high school, avoid unnecessary and difficult science and math courses (goodbye math and physics; hello "rocks for jocks" and introduction to astronomy), and take courses that promise to talk about sex (psychology, sociology).

Academic adventurism is fine when students are comfortable, well prepared, and confident. It is a recipe for boring and safe choices, crowd-following and work avoidance when students are unsure of themselves. That first-year course in Russian or Chinese seems an awful lot more daunting than sticking with familiar turf, like first-year English, French and biology. By giving students almost carte blanche to explore the academy as they see fit, however, universities simply re-enforce conservative and safe choices.

Core (mandatory) courses provide a partial solution to this situation. Universities know what students should learn and they know the kind of courses and programs of study that prepare them well for advanced years. They also know that the average seventeen- or eighteen-year-old is not likely to happen upon the right set of courses by chance. A proper first-year program lays out a sequence of required courses. Some of them may be comprehensive classes that introduce students to the range of disciplines within the academy. McMaster, for example, requires students to take a first-year course called "Inquiry," which canvasses many of the basic disciplines and provides a focused introduction to fundamental university-level skills. UNBC, at its founding, committed five first-year courses to a comprehensive review of the humanities, social sciences, natural sciences, physical sciences, and university communication. There are other variants around. The University of King's College in Halifax has a particularly successful one.

University students need and deserve guidance, particularly at the point of entry. There is no reason why all students cannot get a common core of foundational courses that will serve them well in later years. The University of Manitoba has taken this approach, delaying students' degree choices until they have a solid and full year of studies under their belts. Experimentation and wide-ranging choices require an understanding of options. Few first-year students really understand what sociology or anthropology are, let alone rhetoric, nanotechnology, media studies, communication, gerontology, gender studies, and many other interesting and emerging fields. Universities and university faculty should tell students what they need to know, based on their general area of interest and should provide a narrow set of courses that will provide them with the basic and fundamental skills required for academic success. Abandoning first-year students in this way leads more to nibbling at the edges of new knowledge than it does to deep and thoughtful understanding of the intellectual range of the modern academy.

On the other hand...

The idea of requiring undergraduates to take certain courses, usually in their first year, is a seductive one for academics. You could draw up a number of lists, depending on your world view: a Marxist would have quite a different one than a right-winger. The other idea behind the proposal is that young adults of eighteen are not fit judges of what they ought to know, and should not approach university as though it were a smorgasbord. Rather, they should learn what wiser people tell them to learn, at least for their first year.

This idea has been put into practice at a number of American universities. There are liberal arts colleges where all the first-year students take the same courses. At a number of places, incoming students are required to read a package of material the summer before their first enrolment, and they discuss their reading when they arrive.

It sounds good, but it won't work in this country, except in very limited circumstances. First, there are no purely liberal arts colleges in Canada, so there is almost no student body that would be sympathetic to the idea—King's in Halifax to the contrary notwithstanding. The average student heading for a degree in forestry is not going to be keen on spending an entire year immersed in great ideas rather than in silviculture. This wouldn't matter if universities could compel them, but they can't, which leads to the main reason why the idea won't work: our universities exist in a world where the student as consumer is dominant.

Two generations have gone by since the Hall-Dennis report in Ontario (1968) recommended student-centred learning, and students take their right to choose in education as in most other things as a matter of course. If Canadian universities were hard to get into—if we had universities that had twenty applications for each space—those universities could make students take what courses they liked, as the elite American universities do. But they aren't, and they can't. Students as consumers call the tune, and they want to study what they want. Few universities will dare to buck this fact. UNBC abandoned its core courses. The idea won't work.

76 Academic Fraud Is a Reality

Universities need to be vigilant. This means more than being on the lookout for academic integrity (a nice way of saying cheating). The academy is surrounded by a minefield of fraudulent credentials, fake degrees, and misrepresentation of academic achievements.

In the era of the Internet, where it is quite easy to check on the claims made by public figures, it has become commonplace to discover political candidates and high-profile figures who have overstated their university accomplishments and claimed degrees that they did not earn.

Applications from abroad can pose a particular problem, though most are honest. Institutions receive thousands of applications a year from many nations, from private and public schools, from major centres and little-known towns. Staff in registrar's offices have to identify these institutions, assess them, and review the content of their courses. They then have to convert foreign grades into provincial equivalents to determine eligibility for admission. This takes an enormous amount of effort—some institutions contract out these reviews to private companies—but it is essential if institutions are to maintain their academic standards.

Even such scrutiny does not protect against fraud. In some countries, unscrupulous educational agents take money to ensure that a client's son or daughter gets into a top Canadian school. Sometimes the agent, or someone else, is involved in forging transcripts. Cleverly done—often in the language of the home country and therefore more difficult to verify—they can slip past even the careful review of the admissions clerks. Of course, students unable to succeed at university will fail soon enough, but this is hardly an effective line of defence against such cheating.

If students need a little illicit help once they've been accepted into university, it's easy to find. *The Chronicle of Higher Education* recently carried an article about a man who makes about $60,000 a year writing student papers—not just short undergraduate ones, but long pieces for graduate and professional students. He claims to have written a PhD dissertation in sociology and a Master's degree in cognitive psychology. It's available on-line, and makes for enlightening and depressing reading.

Want a prestigious degree from a top institution? Just include it in your resume—and hope that no one checks. There's little chance they will. In the United States fewer than 20 per cent of employers ask to see university transcripts as part of the hiring process—even universities routinely fail to ask to see a copy of the record of grades and marks of people applying for jobs.

A psychology professor, hired on the basis of an impressive resume, turned out to a complete fraud. A customer had left his resume in the man's taxi and, using the document as leverage, the fraudster managed to get a full-time job at a small Canadian university, even though he'd never attended university at all. It took an entire semester to unmask him. Another individual, eager to find work, submitted her husband's resume to a competition and was awarded a position. As with the psychology professor, who kept talking about "maniac depressives," it was the students who detected her ignorance. Their complaints led to investigations and, eventually, firing.

Fake degrees are widespread around the world, offered through paper institutions that exist only to collect payments and issue diplomas. Other institutions, particularly in the United States, offer degrees on very specious grounds—those that give credit for "life experience" and award a degree for a couple of months' work are particularly popular. One western Canadian professor drew attention to his PhD degree when applying for promotion. A member of the committee checked out the institution that had awarded it, and discovered that it was little more than a mail drop. The faculty member claimed to have been in full-time study for a period of time that overlapped with a summer teaching commitment at another institution. He offered to bring in a copy of his thesis to prove he had earned his degree. Sadly, there was a fire in his garage that week and his documents were lost. He wasn't fired, but he wasn't promoted.

Given the number of universities and colleges in the world—more than 17,000—it's impossible for universities or employers to know about all of them. The very diversity of the system creates openings for fraud. Many of those peddling false information, either to get into an institution or to attract attention and interest in the workplace, will be caught out. When they are discovered, action tends to be decisive and harsh. After all, university degrees are ephemeral and intangible products—the reputation comes from the collective accomplishments of the students and faculty. Trying to gain credibility by association, or trying to claim academic achievements where none exist, undercuts the integrity of the whole system.

77 We Need to Establish Basic Competencies

The student's e-mail was gracious, including glowing comments on her experience at the university, giving her professors full credit for her acceptance into a prestigious graduate school. It was, in all respects save one, the kind of letter that gets circulated widely as a celebration of the faculty's success. The "but" is significant. The e-mail was four paragraphs long and had at least twenty-five grammatical and spelling mistakes. It was, as an example of a graduate's ability to communicate at an advanced professional level, a real embarrassment.

Universities make strong statements about the benefits of an academic degree. Graduates, we promise, will be able to read and write effectively. They will have strong analytical skills, be able to defend their ideas, speak clearly, conduct advanced research using primary and secondary sources, and (in some disciplines) be numerate and able to handle statistical material. It is a long and impressive list, well connected to the skills that employers declare essential for career and personal success.

What we should be saying is that university students have a chance to *gain* these basic competencies, not that they will necessarily *have* these skills when they graduate. Virtually all programs have classes and assignments that test and improve students' general abilities—as well as adding specialized knowledge and discipline-specific skills. Chemistry students learn to work in highly technical laboratories; historians gain insights into how to conduct primary research. Both groups of students should learn to read, write, and participate in debate about disciplinary ideas and concepts.

Alas, the truth is that many students graduate without strong abilities in the core skill areas. In one particularly egregious case, a mature student failed a number of courses (she was required to withdraw from the university on several occasions) until she found professors who were easy graders and didn't care much about writing skills. She took every course they offered, gradually earning enough credits for an Associate's degree (the equivalent of two years study). She still could not write.

With growing class sizes, increased use of part-time instructors, strains on student support services, and heavy demands on professors, universities are not always able to give individual students the focused attention they require. The decline in admission standards at many institutions has also meant that a significant number of students enter universities without the traditional set of academic skills.

Universities must ensure that a degree conveys a specific message about their graduates. Holding a degree from a publicly funded Canadian university should mean that a graduate has each of the basic core competencies at an appropriate level. An English major's numeracy skills may be much lower than a computer science graduate's, but the English student will certainly have far more advanced abilities in literary analysis. Individual programs and faculties should make clear and public commitments to ensuring that these core competencies are taught in a series of required courses. These courses—whether they ask the student to demonstrate appropriate writing, analytical, presentation, or other skills—should operate as gatekeepers for the degree, ensuring that each graduate of the program has the abilities that the university, faculty, and department/program have identified as being integral to it.

Establishing the core competencies, program by program, is a contentious but necessary task. Assigning courses that ensure students have the required, specific skills will be difficult. Equally, universities will have to offer remedial assistance to students who are otherwise doing well in their program but who founder on one of the fundamental requirements. With core competencies defined and embedded in academic programs, and with extra help for students struggling to get over a specific bar, the quality of graduates and the meaning of a university education will improve considerably. A first step involves having a few words with professors who don't care much about writing skills.

A small-business owner called two years ago to complain about a recently hired graduate from the university. This young person had been hired because of his supposed ability to operate in his native language and in English. The position required English-speaking and writing abilities. The student had difficulty making himself understood in English, particularly on the telephone, and could not write at a professional level. "What," asked the employer, "does a degree from your university mean if a graduate cannot handle the most basic of all tasks?" It is a fair question—and one that requires urgent and system-wide attention.

78 A Nationally Uneven System

Ontario, for decades the wealthiest province in Canada, has long been parsimonious with universities. Few people know that Ontario ranks tenth out of ten provinces in funding for universities per student. Expressed on a North American scale (fifty states and ten provinces), Ontario ranks fifty-ninth.

What? A wealthy province, with a set of superb research-intensive universities and a network of access-based institutions ranks lower than Prince Edward Island and Manitoba, and slums with Mississippi near the bottom of the continental rankings? It should be embarrassing, but no one seems embarrassed.

Here's the back story: Federal government equalization payments (until recently Ontario provided billions of dollars for redistribution to the other provinces) provide block funding to the provinces for education, health, and social services. Before the Trudeau era, this money was tied to specific activities and expenditures—so much for health, so much for universities. In 1977 Prime Minister Pierre Trudeau, in an ill-conceived act of appeasement to the provinces, put all of the money into a single pot called the "block funding transfer," and gave the provinces the power to spend it as they wished. The unchecked growth of healthcare spending subsequently ate up an ever-larger portion of this fund, leaving an ever-smaller portion for the university sector.

Provincial governments have different priorities, and they allocate their funds accordingly. The Atlantic provinces, led by Nova Scotia, truly believe in post-secondary education and have walked the talk. Ontario, despite lip service paid by Premier Dalton McGuinty to education and research, sits at the bottom of the pile, well behind big-spending, right-wing Alberta and right behind social democratic nanny state Quebec.

Here are the public funding figures for Canadian universities, per student for 2007–2008 (source: Statistics Canada):

Alberta	$22,469
Saskatchewan	$18,067
Newfoundland and Labrador	$16,169
Manitoba	$13,860
Nova Scotia	$13,552
Prince Edward Island	$13,209
New Brunswick	$13,114
Canada (national average)	$12,500
British Columbia	$12,342
Quebec	$12,006
Ontario	$9,718

The implications here are huge. Dalhousie University, a fine Maritime school, has much smaller class sizes than the University of Waterloo—an equally fine institution but clearly very cost efficient. York University is starved for cash compared to places like the University of Manitoba or Simon Fraser University. The president of a large Ontario university (not Waterloo) observed that his budget would be almost twice the size if his institution was in Alberta. Over time—and Ontario's slide has been pronounced and increasing—the gap between the quality of education, research, and service between the provinces will get wider and wider.

What is odd about the differences between provinces is that they don't follow the standard Canadian pattern. The Atlantic provinces are not the poor children of the post-secondary system in Canada; Ontario holds that distinction. The Government of Ontario argues, with some justification, that the problem lies with the distribution of tax revenue in Canada. It is also true that the allocations reflect provincial priorities. Ontario's top priority is accessibility, not the quality of the educational experience. Equally, the province funds all institutions on the same per-student basis (there is more flexibility with research funding and capital budgets, the latter being closely tied in all provinces to political considerations). Canada is nothing if not committed to full equality.

The distortions are either offset or made worse by donor support and specialized government grants, depending on the success of fundraising drives. British Columbia funds capital projects separately from the per student grants. Ontario occasionally has time-limited allocations for major buildings, but universities are also expected to pay for buildings through their annual budgets. The result—evident to anyone who visits campuses in the two provinces—is aesthetically pleasing buildings in British Columbia, functionality and frugality in Ontario.

For many decades, the distinctive characteristic of Canada's university system was its uniform quality. The University of New Brunswick is a terrific university, despite the province's lower standard of living. Alberta's long-term prosperity did not automatically ensure a better system. This pattern is now very much at risk, and significant changes are starting to show up. In this respect, Canada will be moving closer to the American model of public education, where there are substantial differences between and even within states. Given the nature of federal-provincial relations—and Quebec's jealous stranglehold on all matters educational makes significant changes extremely difficult—it is highly unlikely that a national solution will be found.

It's safe to say that the gap between rich and poor will accelerate and that differences based on quality and resources will increasingly become a feature of the Canadian university system. As we argue elsewhere, this is not necessarily a bad thing, but it's certainly not the traditional Canadian way of doing things.

Quebec's Absurd Fee Policy

Quebec, even more than Alberta, is the classic Canadian outlier. It loves to do its own thing. And its universities are no exception. The province has a CEGEP system, essentially combining Grade 12 and first-year university into a transition program from high school to post-secondary studies. It maintains the only truly provincial network of universities—the Université de Québec, with ten campuses across the province. It supports both English and French institutions (as does Ontario, by the way, particularly through York University's Glendon College and the bilingual University of Ottawa and Laurentian University). But it is on the tuition front that Quebec really stands apart.

Under the influence of the powerful student and faculty unions, Quebec has resisted the temptation to increase tuition fees to keep up with rising university costs. Result: Quebec's university fees are the lowest in the country, around $2,000 per year for an Arts degree (for residents of the province) compared to a national average of around $5,000. The provincial government is ideologically wedded to the (very bad) idea of keeping university fees artificially low, believing it is central to its goal of achieving broad accessibility. When the province's leading business schools sought to raise their fees to allow them to compete—principally for top scholars—with English Canadian and American schools, the government closed off the option. The authorities even indicated that they would claw back from the government grant to the university any additional income earned from higher fees.

Quebec's low tuition fees have been a failure. The province has the second-lowest university participation rate in Canada, and by quite some distance. The provinces with the highest fees have the highest participation rates, a disquieting result that flies in the face of student and Quebecois assertions about the impact of tuition fees. So students get a cheap ride and threaten to take to the streets in protest at the slightest sign of tuition reform or increases. The provincial government—knowing only too well from the history of the post-1960 era the role of the academy in political protests and the separatist movement—is afraid to antagonize a potentially formidable foe. It opts for the easy solution, one that hamstrings Quebec institutions, subsidizes the wealthiest families in the province, and doesn't promote broad university participation.

But Quebec has allowed higher tuition fees in other areas. Again standing apart from Canadian norms the province allows the universities to charge higher fees for out-of-province Canadian students (and higher fees again for international students). A Montreal student enrolled at Concordia will pay $2,000 for a first-year Arts program; a student from Edmunston, across the border in New Brunswick, pays $5,600; and an international student pays $18,000. No other province charges higher fees for out-of-province Canadian students, for it undercuts one of the core principles of Canadian federalism: the transferability of social benefits. The policy has not raised any public outcry, largely because of the country's reluctance to stir up Quebecois reaction. It's outrageous, of course, but that's the kind of country we live in.

Quebec itself is the major loser here. Its fee structure is a significant disincentive for Canadians from other provinces. At a time when thousands of young Canadians graduate each year from French-immersion programs, you'd think Quebec would be delighted to welcome these French-speaking students to their province. Quebec's birthrate is plunging, it is desperately searching for immigrants, and it is encouraging childbearing among the Quebecois. The province ought to be encouraging students with French-language skills to come to Quebec. Instead of drawing other Canadians to the province's universities, Quebec encourages them to stay away. Bad for Quebec, bad for Canada.

Almost Everyone Is Eligible

There was a time, a couple of generations ago, when it was tough for the ordinary eighteen-year-old to get into university. Not so today. In fact it's quite easy—even for the academically challenged and sluggishly motivated—to find a place that will accept them, provided they aren't too picky about where they go. As long as students are flexible they will find that many universities aren't too choosy about who they let in. Even with close to half of all high school graduates going to a post-secondary institution, the country has long since passed the point where students have to fight for a spot, somewhere.

In Canada, the expansion of the university system began with the belief that every eligible and interested student deserved a chance to attend a post-secondary institution. That was a noble goal, so long as "eligible" meant "meeting a high standard." But from the 1960s onward, the definition began to be debased. By the 1970s, universities began to play the same role in society that high schools had played during the 1930s and 1940s. They became finishing schools for the masses, a place to grow, mature, and make a gentle transition to both adulthood and the rough world of work. By the start of the twenty-first century, Canada had one of the highest post-secondary participation rates and graduation rates among the leading industrialized nations.

Entrance standards, inevitably, have dropped, as universities have lowered the standards required for admission. One dramatic statistic illustrates this process, a statistic that should quell any doubt that grade inflation in high schools really exists. About fifty years ago, Ontario introduced a program to recognize "Ontario Scholars." Students who got an average of 80 per cent in their final year of high school (then Grade 13, now Grade 12) received this designation, and a grant of several hundred dollars. In the early days, 3 to 5 per cent of graduating students achieved this average—a phenomenal accomplishment, given that nine separate exams were involved and standards were high. By 2010, however, the 3 per cent had ballooned to nearly 50. It's possible of course that Ontario students are a great deal smarter (or better taught) in 2010 than they were in 1960, but it's far more likely that grade inflation has sucked much of the meaning out of high school grades.

More than half of Canadian universities appear to accept all students who meet the minimum qualifications, qualifications that have become increasingly easy to achieve. Several years back, almost all students in Saskatchewan who met the bar at the University of Saskatchewan or the University of Regina were admitted. And campuses such as Winnipeg, Brandon, St. Thomas, UNBSJ, Cape Breton University, Memorial University at Cornerbrook, Lakehead, and other places followed suit. The students did not necessarily get into the program of their choice—nursing is more selective than arts, business has more applicants than science—but they got in and then had the chance to switch majors and areas of study once they were on campus.

By the late 1990s the expansion of the Canadian university had met a primary objective: virtually all Canadian students could, if they were willing to move, find a place at a Canadian university.

The "Man" Problem at Our Universities

Universities used to belong to men. In 1959 there were 3.25 men for every female undergraduate, and 5.5 men for every female graduate student in Canada. The smaller number of women who attended universities clustered in "traditional" programs like nursing, English literature, languages, and home economics. Elementary school teachers, most of them women, did not need a degree before the 1960s. There were enough women around— searching (in the sexist vernacular of the time) for their "Mrs. Degree"—to ensure that campus life was sociable and civilized. But the universities were male. In 1971, 60 per cent of all university degrees were awarded to men, and virtually all the engineering, math, law, business, medicine, and science degrees went to them.

How much and how fast the tables have turned. By 2006, 63 per cent of Canadian university degrees went to women. In the same year, 57 per cent of all undergraduates enrolled full time (61 per cent part time) were women, which suggests they have a higher completion rate than men. The numbers seem to have levelled off. The balance is not shifting any further towards women (in 2008 they earned 60 per cent of degrees)—but men are not yet making a comeback within the academy. In 2008–2009, of the 1.12 million university students in Canada (full and part time), 471,000 were men and 640,000 were women. The 2010 *Maclean's* report on Canadian universities noted that at twenty-four of them, at least 60 per cent of the students were female.

At most Canadian medical schools, more women than men are studying to be doctors. Veterinarian medicine and pharmacy programs are attracting more women than men, and law schools—once the last preserve of the alpha male—are seeing more and more young women. Women still dominate fields like nursing, education, the humanities, and languages. But men do still hold a firm grip on the hard sciences, including mathematics, computer science, and engineering.

The academic success of young women is showing up across most of the university system. This is particularly true of Caucasian women, for males of Asian background are considerably keener about university than young men from traditional English and French backgrounds. It's not quotas or special arrangements that have allowed women to equal and even surpass men in many academic and professional areas. The women do well in hotly contested areas mostly because they study and work harder than men do. Or perhaps, as some have suggested, their brains are better wired for book learning.

Women are more likely to graduate from high school than men. They are more likely to go to university. They are more likely to graduate. They are at least as likely and, in a growing number of cases, more likely to get into the elite professional schools. Look at the lists of scholarship winners at high school and university graduations. There are lots of talented and hard-working men on the list, but in many instances, the number of women outstrips their percentage of the school population.

Now, this would not be a big problem if it turns out that men have simply found a different path to training, career success, and happiness. Maybe, as some have suggested, men simply figured out earlier than women that there is a declining return on investment for university education. If so, they should dominate the colleges and trade schools. But they don't, for much the same pattern of "women rising" can be seen in college programs, apprenticeships, and even the paid workforce. The young men are not at university, nor are they showing up at other educational and training programs either.

In the past, even this would not have been a crisis. Fifty years ago, male high school graduates or dropouts could find a good job in the factory, the lumber camp, with a trucking company, or in the oil patch. But most of these opportunities are gone, victims of outsourcing, global competition, the failure of Canadian competitiveness or, most of all, technological innovation. In the twenty-first century, low-skilled jobs for men means working in the service sector, where they find themselves competing for work with university graduates.

Now you can see the real problem. Men are not going to university in the expected numbers. They are not graduating with great career prospects. And the old default jobs—unskilled work—are declining in significance. The potential impact of the new realities on patterns of partnerships, child-rearing, and the like could be considerable. Professions such as medicine and law will have to adapt to new gender realities. It appears that women practice medicine differently than men do. They spend more time, for example, with each patient and are less focused on producing income than their male counterparts are. Estimates indicate that it takes three female doctors to cover the clinical practices of two male doctors (although patient satisfaction is higher). The legal profession is struggling to balance its work- and billing-obsessed culture with respect for child rearing and the desire of many female lawyers for a more sustainable work-life balance.

There's an added twist. It's long been common for professional men to marry less-educated women: the doctor marries the nurse, the executive the secretary, the lawyer the schoolteacher. It's less common for well-educated, accomplished women to marry less-educated men.

Perhaps Men Are Right

So, what happens to the young men who, in large and growing numbers, are not doing well in school, have trouble finding high-paying, stable jobs and a marriage partner, and don't seem to fit into the service-oriented twenty-first century economy?

We're in the midst of finding out. One segment of Canadian society— First Nations people—provides a grim warning. First Nations women are far more likely to go to university than men. Once educated, they tend to stay in urban centres and often marry outside their First Nation. The young men, in turn, are educationally disenfranchised, without work or prospects, and often live in communities where many of the most talented, well-educated and active women have left. They often feel they have no future. The result? Frustration, anger, abuse, and self-destructive behaviour.

Elsewhere in Canadian society many families know exactly where these young men have gone. When you tell an audience that you have found the missing young men—they are in their parents' basements playing video games and working just enough to keep themselves in male toys—the bitter laughter from a sizable portion of the audience lets you know you are right. Add to this the reality of boomerang children—kids who return home after a period of time of near independence—and you have pinpointed one of the most serious generational challenges of the early twenty-first century.

Put some numbers to this trend and you realize that it's not a marginal statistical problem. The situation is already startling—at some institutions, the student body is close to 70 per cent female. Ontario estimates suggest that by the 2020s there will be 91,000 more women than men in the provincial university system. In short order there will be many more women in the professional workforce than men. The women are likely to find a receptive job market, for the collapse in the low-skill, high-wage "male" work of the 1960s and 1970s has been matched by the growth of opportunity in the social and health services, including nursing, geriatrics, and the like.

Many men need a university education, and universities require men. Yet very little is being done about this situation, nor in most places is it even discussed. We've hardly begun to look into why so few young men are in our classrooms. High schools have to figure out why males are tuning out and ignoring the challenges of scholarship and personal development. The change is so recent, so dramatic, and so unexpected that universities have not yet been able to respond.

Could it be that there is, in fact, no problem? It's simply that men have decided that university degrees are not worth the effort required to earn them? Young men, so it is said, are more focused on career and income, they have listened closely to the growing chatter about the poor career options of university graduates—the jokes about English graduates asking, "will you have fries with that?" Maybe women are deluding themselves, while the young men know more than the system does, and realize that a university degree is not a ticket to success. If so, maybe the absence of men simply means they have made wiser choices about their education than women have. But clearly the imbalance in the professional programs, at least, is worrying.

If the problem exists, what is to be done? First, universities and governments have to acknowledge the issue. Second, we need to know a lot more about the background and reasons for the dramatic shift. Third, university recruiting needs to be adjusted to speak directly to the young men, and it must address their reasons for avoiding the academy. Universities need to collaborate with colleges and employers to determine what is needed to attract young men to post-secondary and career-training opportunities. Fourth, parents need to be brought into the equation. They need to be mobilized to work with high school teachers and counsellors to ensure that young men understand the problems that await them if they do not prepare themselves properly for a career.

Finally, universities need to determine if their program mix, teaching style, or lack of perceived relevance is keeping young men away and—if the system is partially or substantially at fault—must adjust their operations to attract, retain, and graduate more young men.

Don't Mock the Social Sciences

Have you noticed that when politicians and the public criticize universities, they typically take aim at the social sciences and humanities? Commentators love to make fun of English, political science, education, and cultural studies, but they give engineering, physics, and chemistry a wide berth. Back when the Reform Party aimed its populist guns at the academy, MPs routinely rose in the House of Commons to mock federal funding of some odd-sounding humanities or social science research project. Hardly ever did they make fun of science-based projects (though on one memorable occasion, Reformers drew the nation's attention to a biology project related to the production of blackberry or blueberry jam—one MP offered to introduce the scientist to his grandmother).

Critics steer clear of the sciences and applied sciences for a variety of reasons. First, few people understand exactly what the scientists are doing. It's easy to say—even if it's wrong—that there is no social merit in researching the emergence of gay culture on the Prairies, or deconstructing depictions of gender relations in Shakespearean plays. It's much harder to decide if a project on distributed embedded real-time systems, or research on the fundamental interactions of small molecules (such as substrates and drugs) with enzymes warrants federal funding.

The sciences and applied sciences have won the relevance contest hands down, even if that widely shared judgment is not really fair. Engineers build things, and they seem to be contributing directly to economic development. High-speed Internet technologies, solar cars, new welding systems—these all seem directly applicable to the present day. Scientists also tackle "real world" stuff—climate change, water pollution, genetic testing, the transmission of disease, the cause of memory loss, and the creation of new drugs. But the truth is, there are just as many esoteric, curiosity driven, and weird-seeming research projects in the sciences as in the social sciences and humanities. And that is precisely how it should be. Some of this work is not directly applicable to contemporary problems, but there is nothing in the social sciences and humanities that matches the search for the origins of the universe in pure public interest (no visiting humanities scholar has ever attracted the nationwide interest accorded Stephen Hawking in the summer of 2010).

There are just as many directly applicable and highly relevant social science and humanities research initiatives as there are in the sciences and applied sciences. Historians study the nature of the residential school movement and work with lawyers to resolve land claims. Political scientists try to explain the drop in voter participation and look for ways to bring more citizens to the voting booths. Economists explore the origins of the recent financial crisis and look for regulatory mechanisms to prevent a recurrence. Sociologists examine the relationship between religion and terrorism, and psychologists try to figure out how governments can stop people from smoking. Linguists find new ways to teach second languages, and cultural studies specialists look at how video games are affecting social relations and children's involvement with the education system.

It's true, many humanities and social science projects address questions internal to the disciplines and are not of immediate interest to the public at large, but a great deal of effort is being made by these researchers—just as with scientists and applied scientists—to address practical and contemporary problems.

It's too bad that the sciences and applied sciences capture the public's imagination in a way that the humanities and social sciences are rarely able to do. So try a little test. Grab a piece of paper and, on one side, write down the top five or ten things that worry you most in the world. On the other side, write down the same number of things that bring you the greatest pleasure. The answers are pretty consistent. On the worry side, the answers typically include responding to climate change, terrorism, the prospect of economic collapse, political uncertainty, religious conflict, globalization, coping with rapid technological change, and maintaining a sustainable health care system. On the positive side, people generally identify their family, their church, music, theatre, movies, love/romance, sex, literature, friends/community, shopping, recreation, and the like. Now, go back over these lists and circle all of the ones that are studied by social scientists and humanities people. Almost everything has been circled. What a powerful illustration of the importance of the social sciences and humanities!

Universities—and societies—need the sciences, applied sciences, social sciences, and humanities (and the fine and performing arts). Creating a conflict between the various university disciplines is both counterproductive and wrong. The sciences are in the ascendancy at present, largely because they (and the medical professions) have learned to play the public and politicians like a well-tuned fiddle. Social scientists and humanities specialists, perhaps because they assume what they do is self-evident, have made less effort and been less successful in alerting the public and governments to the value of their work, largely because they promote the freedom of individual faculty members and the importance of curiosity-driven research over work designed to address precise and pressing societal issues. They have a great deal to learn from their colleagues in the sciences and applied sciences.

The University Myth

The whole world is university-crazy. Only a few decades ago, universities were comparatively rare around the world and largely served the economic and social elite. Now, universities are exploding in number and diversity around the globe. There may be more than 100 million students in universities, and all but the most destitute and crisis-ridden countries are making substantial investments in university education. Countries are racing to educate their youth, all believing that a highly educated workforce is crucial to national success.

The only thing missing in this assumption is evidence. University education is a wonderful and remarkable gift. Ideally, the chance to study at university would be available to all who wish to go and have the talent and motivation to succeed. But the implicit assumption that this wonderful education will guarantee personal and national success needs to be carefully examined.

University education originally gained a high market value mainly because of its exclusivity. In times when most students did not graduate from high school, holding a university degree was a mark of real distinction. In 1961, only about 5 per cent of Canadians of all ages held university degrees. In 1971 it was about 17 per cent, and by 2006 about 23 per cent. Now, when high school graduation rates are very high, the university degree is almost ubiquitous. Similarly, countries with strong and well-functioning university systems used to have a distinct advantage over the rest of the world. The leadership in university education of the United Kingdom, Germany, and the United States in the nineteenth and twentieth centuries helped fuel national development on all social, political, economic, and cultural fronts. Countries that lagged behind—throughout Asia, the Middle East, Latin America (with exceptions such as Argentina and Brazil at times), and Africa—seemed destined to remain poor.

But the world is catching up and, in some quarters, racing ahead. China—with fewer than a million undergraduates as recently as 1997—now has more than eight million students studying at more than 2,500 public and private institutions. Even if we accept (and be careful here) the stereotype of the Chinese student as narrowly trained, uncritical, and unoriginal, the sheer size and scope of the Chinese system will produce a steadily increasing number of superb graduates. Add to this the amazing growth of university education in India—where some of the most competitive institutions in the world can be found—and many other countries, and you'll realize that the West's educational advantage is dead, or at least dying.

But are our core assumptions about a university education correct? When politicians and educational advocates speak of the great value of a university education, they are right to talk about the mind-expanding, context-providing, skills-producing aspects. But other claims are disingenuous. There is enormous demand for certain university graduates—in Canada it is generally limited to the medical professions, some branches of engineering, and a few emerging technical areas—and limited demand in most others. At the same time employers are screaming for IT technicians, specialized technical personnel, millwrights, plumbers, electricians, and other applied fields. Unemployment rates among university graduates— and the almost equally depressing underemployment rates—are creeping up in the Western world. In the developing world, where people assume there is a huge demand for highly trained people, unemployment among university graduates has also become a serious problem. A 2009 report indicated that nearly 30 per cent of China's university graduates, during a time of unprecedented economic growth, could not find work. There were more unemployed Chinese graduates in 2007—almost 1 million—than there were university students in all of Canada.

Success can be a two-edged sword. If we convince governments to expand universities—and parents to pay for their children's attendance—we produce many more universities, literally tens of millions more students around the world, and a steady decline in the status and economic value of most university degrees. The very enthusiasm for expanding the university system globally may, ironically, put a serious damper on government, parental, and eventually student enthusiasm for the investment of time and money in an advanced education.

None of this diminishes the personal and intellectual value of a properly earned university degree. But the reality certainly calls into question the legitimacy of assuming continued exponential growth in undergraduate education. There is a very good chance the world will catch on to a basic truth: the golden opportunities awaiting university graduates are not infinite.

85 Will Universities Lead the Innovation Economy?

Governments are taking quite a gamble. They're pouring money into university research, hoping it will lay the foundation for twenty-first century economic prosperity.

From Botswana to Japan, from Finland to Taiwan, governments and their academic partners have bought into a widely shared belief that investments in basic scientific and technological research will spark economic development and growth. Huge investments in major research facilities—university laboratories, faculty researchers, and technicians—are now commonplace. The people behind the $9 billion Large Hadron Collider started lobbying for the next piece of high-tech equipment within months of its opening. Headhunting competition for scientists, typically raided from each other's laboratories, has become an international blood sport, with China and Korea fuelling a global race for talent. The argument about the commercial value of scientific and technical research is compelling, for there are clear successes—like Silicon Valley in California, Boston, and Waterloo in Canada.

But is it true? First, academic research generally translates poorly into commercial products. Very few patents, processes, or products that emerge from university laboratories make it to market. Second, university research laboratories and classrooms are rarely the birthplaces of entrepreneurs. There are some, to be sure, but university faculty who convert their academic achievements into commercial successes are few and far between. They are, after all, academics, pursuing research driven by curiosity and supported by peer-reviewed grants. Much the same is true of technology transfer offices, patent protection assistance, and other government and university-supported mechanisms for producing commercial success.

Instead, there is growing belief around the world that informal contact— in coffee shops and the like—between researchers and entrepreneurs is the best means of promoting commercialization. Equally, students functioning in dynamic, cutting-edge environments are often inspired to leave the limitations of the academy to pursue their commercial ideas. Many of the key people in the dot.com revolution—Bill Gates, Steve Jobs, and others—did not find universities good environments for their work and aspirations.

Science has advanced enormously through the investments in the innovation agenda. There are more and better-funded laboratories than ever. The frontiers of science and technology are being moved back rapidly. Indeed, the movement of scientific knowledge well outstrips both the efforts at commercialization and society's capacity to understand and accept change, as the experiences of nanotechnology and biotechnology demonstrate. There is more money for graduate students and for new equipment.

But innovation may kill as many jobs as it creates. A combination of market forces and technological changes has gutted the logging industry in British Columbia in recent years, eliminating many more jobs than have been created by the expansion of high-tech sectors. Improvements in robotics have allowed companies to eliminate jobs in manufacturing, just as Computer Assisted Drawing technology has resulted in mass layoffs in drafting and related fields, and computer worksheets have transformed the need for workers in the accounting areas.

Innovation is not an automatic boon to regional and national prosperity, although companies that fail to keep abreast of technological developments can find themselves uncompetitive extremely quickly. What's more, there's no assurance that innovations will remain within the region or country that spawned them. A researcher at a particular university is not compelled to bring her product or idea to market in that area or even that nation. Most universities lay claim to some portion of the financial return from such commercial developments (though the University of Waterloo leaves complete control of the intellectual property with the creator). But returns from this source are very small. Indeed in Canada, very little commercial development actually stays here. Most is sold at pre-development or early-stage development to companies outside Canada. In fact, Canadian taxpayers may be paying for economic growth in other countries.

There is a huge and sad irony in the relationship between innovation and university research. There are key areas where research might well contribute substantially to the creation of innovative, creative, and expanding economies. This research would come from the social sciences and humanities—areas that have been largely left out of the explosion of innovation research. There are some great researchers working in the field, but they pale by comparison—in number and resources—with the science and technology areas. There are many unanswered questions about the creation and maintenance of innovation societies. How does creativity relate to commercialization? Which forms of education best support industrial and economic innovation? What impact do community structure, multiculturalism, and local heritage have on innovation? Which policies best support, or retard, innovation? It's odd that the non-science fields have not been more fully engaged in the study of innovation, but not totally unexpected given the way that social science and humanities research have been marginalized at most universities.

Mike Lazaridis, co-CEO of Research In Motion and one of Canada's leading supporters of academic research, described university convocations as "the best technology transfer process around." Although he spent a hundred million dollars of his own money to support basic research in theoretical physics and quantum computing, he did not think universities were innovation engines by themselves. Rather, he argued, the training of bright young people, unleashed into the world as employers and entrepreneurs, was the single greatest means of promoting commercial innovation and economic prosperity. Effective use of the classroom, to Lazaridis, is the best way of ensuring Canadian prosperity.

Universities Are Like Post Offices

In 1984, in a book called *The Great Brain Robbery*, two Canadian history professors suggested that universities were, in the late twentieth century, what post offices were in the nineteenth. At that time the post office was the only physical presence of government in the community in small towns across the country. Like post offices, universities now show that the government cares about the local citizenry and is willing to spend money to provide the region's children with the opportunity to pursue their education dreams and career ambitions.

In the late 1950s, most Canadian universities were in large cities. Only a handful—Bishop's, St. Francis Xavier, Mount Alison, and Acadia—operated in smaller communities. But by the early twenty-first century almost every community in the country with a population of more than 50,000 hosted a university or a branch campus, and many smaller centres also had a community college close at hand. Just like the post office.

Who would have thought in 1960 that fifty years later there would be universities in Sydney, North Bay, Rimouski, Kelowna, and Prince George, a University College in Thompson, a satellite law program from the University of Victoria operating in Iqaluit, and Alaskan MBA courses offered in Whitehorse?

On Vancouver Island university-level courses are offered not only in Victoria by its university and its college, but at universities and colleges in Duncan, Nanaimo, Courtenay, Qualicum, Parksville, Powell River (on the mainland), Campbell River, Port Alberni, and Port Hardy. In other words, virtually every community is served, and no one on this large island lives beyond an easy commute to the nearest campus. And in BC as a whole practically every community of any size now has a post-secondary institution either in or near it. Just like the post office.

If We Ran the University

If we were made "University Dictator" for a year, here are ten things we would do:

1. Give presidents real power. At present presidents operate as persuasive leaders, but without real authority since their power is so limited by senates and boards of governors. Large, complex institutions being buffeted by the forces of change need effective and empowered leaders.

2. Change the current tenure system. Academic freedom must be protected at all costs and these guarantees (many provided by the Charter of Rights and Freedoms) have to be entrenched. We

would also give new faculty members permanent jobs at the point of hiring. In exchange, institute five-year reviews so that weak performers—as defined by colleagues, not administrators—are encouraged to find jobs elsewhere.

3. Separate purely professional programs—business, education, and social work are good possibilities—into free-standing and allied institutions. These programs provide very valuable services and work extremely closely with professional organizations and accrediting agencies. The fit within the university system is not always ideal, however, and parallel status would better allow all programs to achieve their potential.

4. Reduce the number of students attending university without cutting the budget for the institution. Cut class sizes, reduce the number of unmotivated students, and ensure that those in attendance truly want to be there.

5. Separate the instructional and research budgets of the university. While encouraging all academics to remain active in their fields, put additional resources into areas of institutional strength and regional/national need. Research centres and institutes have a key role to play in building the profile of Canadian research.

6. Institute an admission test, and use high school grades as only one (a minor) part of the selection criteria. Place greater emphasis on writing and reading ability, reasoning skills, and extracurricular activities.

7. Streamline collegial processes, making sure that faculty members remain in control of crucial academic decisions. Build decision-making structures that encourage speed and flexibility and encourage faculty members to be more outward looking in their approach to their work.

8. Find a wealthy donor willing to fund the construction of a truly impressive university building to demonstrate the fundamental importance of architecture in the creation and maintenance of a learning environment.

9. Double tuition fees (remember they are tax deductible in parents' hands), using one-third of the money to subsidize tuition for low-income students, one-third as an income contingent option for particularly promising students, and the other third to improve campus life, recreation, student facilities, residence spaces, and cultural activities on campus.

10. Create a common first-year program for all students, focusing on basic academic and professional skills, and offering the foundations of a strong general education. Emphasize high-quality teaching and direct student contact with top professors. Build genuine academic excitement into the courses and ensure that all students learn—in their first year—the fundamentals of science, math, technology, fine arts, humanities, and the social sciences.

88 The Mandate for Universities Is Confusing

What seems so simple—universities are designed to provide high-quality teaching and research—has been complicated by changing government expectations and the demands of society. Governments have given universities contradictory and unachievable mandates. As well as teaching and conducting research, universities are now expected to:

- Promote and underpin regional economic development.
- Provide accessibility for local students.
- Offer remedial assistance for students at risk or people with significant academic deficiencies.
- Accept responsibility for responding to new social requirements. In recent years this has included providing more assistance to students with learning and physical disabilities, supporting Aboriginal students, adjusting academic programs to respond to issues of gender, sexuality, ethnicity, and the like.
- Promote the commercialization of academic research, spawning new businesses and supporting industrial growth.
- Support cultural and artistic activity.
- Encourage civic engagement and citizenship.
- Represent the community/region at the national and international level.

These and other challenges are formidable and important. Universities are funded to provide educational opportunities—and they use a good portion of the funding to foster research activity. New responsibilities, added irregularly and rarely with sufficient funding, have skewed institutional life, placed enormous pressure on university administrators, and made faculty jobs much more difficult. They have left universities with a profound sense of being overwhelmed.

Popular Culture Distorts Our Perception of University Life

Movies, television, and novels have given us a distorted notion of what university life is like. Years ago the film *Animal House* celebrated, in a perverse way, the youth culture of the modern academy, just as *The Paper Chase* dramatized the intense intellectual and professional challenges of law school. Colleges and universities are classic fare for American television and movies, producing an image of engagement, challenge, social relationships, and personal development that reinforces the North American preoccupation with attending university. (Deans, understandably, fare very poorly in the popular media, generally coming across as bumbling incompetents, ferocious taskmasters, or perverted bureaucrats.)

Occasionally they give us glimpses inside the classroom—we saw Indiana Jones on the podium briefly—but most focus on the hedonistic lifestyles of college students in the dorms, sororities, and fraternities. Slasher films and murder mysteries are fairly common. Romances, like the tearjerker *Love Story*, are standard fare. In general, the television programs and movies show kids having fun, stressing out over their studies (but leaving the homework to a small number of geeks and Math students), fighting with the establishment, and using the experience to put distance between themselves, their high school past, and their parents.

Less well known is the raunchy pornography of the distressingly successful *Girls Gone Wild* series of videos and DVDs. There is an odd Canadian twist to this phenomenon. Most of the girls—and most are claimed to be college and university students—are "discovered" in bars or parties. Since Canada has a lower drinking age than most American states, the series promoters discovered a terrific opportunity in this country to attract more of the legal-age eighteen-year-olds who were particularly popular among series subscribers.

Canadian media pay much less attention to the university experience, with one major exception. *The Decline of the American Empire*, Denys Arcand's biting and brilliant portrayal of life in a Quebec university history department, has no English-Canadian counterpart. There are glimpses of the academy in the work of a few of our novelists—notably Robertson Davies—but these are infrequent and have not penetrated the public consciousness. There is, in fact, no Canadian variant of the popular culture image-making of the United States. So, in typical Canadian fashion, we expropriate and absorb the American version, which has the effect of idealizing the American experience and making Canada's schools seem drab and uninteresting by comparison.

The Death of the Holistic University Experience

A long time ago, the university experience was a neat package: four years of study and fun—the hallowed halls, the kindly but dotty profs, the attractive dating and marriage prospects, first-year initiations, fraternities, sororities, beer, football, graduation—all of it. This is still the way some people think of college life, but if the university experience was ever like this, it won't be much longer.

The reality of the university system is that it's fragmenting in important ways. Students can get degrees at colleges and from on-line institutions inside and outside Canada. They often work half time or more while studying—so much for the all-in experience of being a student. Participation in campus events is down, many students still live at home, faculty are preoccupied with research and service and have less time for their students. Indeed, they appear on campus a great deal less than before, or are spending more time in their laboratories. And so many students are ill prepared, they often find themselves seeking remedial help and learning basic skills while trying to keep up with university-level content.

The traditional approach to a university education—finish high school, enroll in college, complete a degree, and then move into the workforce—has been replaced by educational anarchy. Some students take time off before coming to university. Others spend time in college and then shift. They finish university and then go to a college for practical study. They continue their work at the graduate or professional school level. They drop out, as much for financial and personal reasons as academic ones, and find work or travel. They switch majors and move between universities. In commuter schools, they often spend much of their university careers with high school friends. On campuses with large numbers of international students, students tend to socialize in separate spheres. Bonding and international exchange rarely happens—though, thankfully, romance remains alive and manages to leap cultural barriers.

New educational institutions are emerging to respond to changing realities. Some places have expanded on-line and distance learning. Private institutes are popping up, offering both on-line and face-to-face instruction. Universities have lost a big portion of the adult learner market to for-profit programs. They are no longer the only show in town on the advanced educational front. The same holds true for discovery and innovation. A great deal of research has shifted off campus, to think-tanks, private companies, government agencies, and other institutions. Journalists and freelance writers are more likely to write provocative books and articles than academics. In many ways, universities are no longer in the forefront of places that are generating the big ideas and challenges to the status quo.

The university system has changed—and we believe the shifts are both profound and permanent. The cloistered, safe, and systematic environment of the past—with students, faculty, and staff sharing in a common campus life experience that sparked life-changing learning and original research—can still be seen in places, even on the biggest campuses. But the fragmentation of the lives of students and faculty has been like a rock hitting the windshield of a speeding car. We can still see ahead, but the cracks in the university system are growing as fast as a windshield star in minus-forty-degree weather. Our collective vision of what universities are, and what they should be, is being obscured and our view of the way forward is getting very blurry. Canadians cling to the old view of what a university should be because it is familiar and comforting. But it's not a view that's consistent with the realities of the early twenty-first century.

VIII

Are Canada's Universities Ready for the Twenty-First Century?

Canada Needs More Science and Technology Graduates

There's a growing belief that global competitiveness is defined largely by university attendance and graduation rates. We think that is wrong. University education has expanded enormously in the last fifty years, yet the greatest growth spurt is still in the offing as China, South Asia, and Africa come fully on stream. It is an article of faith that university education equals economic competitiveness—an argument that Cuba, with a remarkable level of post-secondary participation and graduation, seems to disprove. The issue is not, "are producing enough university graduates?" but, "are we producing enough graduates in the right fields?" It doesn't help that the definition of "right fields" shifts each decade. It makes academic nimbleness a prerequisite for ongoing economic success.

This may sound like an odd argument from a pair of historians. We believe that all students—regardless of their areas of interest—benefit enormously from the insights and abilities associated with the humanities, social sciences, and fine arts. We would like nothing more than to see all students exposed to more arts courses, just as we would like arts students to be exposed more to the science and technological fields. There are enormous advantages in having a broadly educated citizenry and in ensuring that all university graduates have a strong understanding of social, cultural, political, moral, artistic, and economic realities.

But universities have accepted—even pushed—the argument that they play an essential role in ensuring national competitiveness. Companies beg for additional graduates in the "hot" fields and pressure governments to expand opportunities. In some countries—India is the best example—places in the top schools are allocated on two criteria: the students' abilities and national need. In Canada the top priority is student choice. Sure, there are caps on the most popular programs, but given that universities use application numbers to lobby for more funding and to determine aspects of internal allocations, these tend to be short-term.

So Canada has got roughly the university system the students want—which we think is very different from the university system the country needs. We'll end up with the world that analyst Rick Miner described as "People Without Jobs, Jobs Without People." Colleges generally do a much better job of responding to market realities—opening, dropping, expanding, or contracting programs as the employment situation dictates. Universities change more slowly, particularly in the areas of faculty hiring and program development, which makes them much less responsive.

It's clear that the twenty-first century will be dominated by rapid innovations in science and technology, and will present many possibilities in medicine, genetics, biotechnology, nanotechnology, clean technologies and the like. If Canadian universities are to remain competitive they will have to prepare more of the right kind of graduates. This requires a much stronger emphasis on engineering, a shift from the basic sciences to the applied sciences, and greater interdisciplinary study. The combined arts and science degrees offered at universities such as the University of New Brunswick and McMaster are already highly popular and successful. They will be classic twenty-first century degrees.

Universities will also have to adapt in two other ways. First, they'll have to work more closely with employers, both public and private, and build experience learning into more of their programs. Direct connections with the workplace will be essential if the country is to match opportunities and human resources. Second, they will have to think and plan much more quickly. New programs (many of them a year or two in length and built off basic foundational studies) will have to be developed faster—within months instead of years—and they will likely operate for a short period of time. The future will see fewer degrees like Bachelor of Science in Biology and more Bachelor of Biology (Genetic Modelling) and Bachelor of Biology (Environmental Remediation).

We can hear our colleagues in the arts screaming at us already. Not to worry: their disciplines will always have a crucial role to play in the university and society as a whole. Ironically, limiting the number of places in the arts will actually make them more competitive and likely produce stronger students and better graduates. Be brave, colleagues, and remember that what is at stake here is the economic competitiveness and viability of the country.

92 Universities Need a New Funding Model

Most of the money universities *receive*—tuition fees and government grants for students—is tied to teaching activity. More than half of the money they *spend* is associated with research, professional service, and outreach. Does that sound fair?

If universities want to pay faculty higher salaries, hire more professors, expand research activity, or develop new outreach initiatives they either have to pry more money out of government, or take in more students. Specialized grant funding covers the marginal costs of new projects—hiring more lab or research assistants, paying for conference travel and field research, and the like. But the core costs of a university—largely faculty salaries, library holdings, and research facilities—come from the income derived from student enrolment. (There is an exception—the so-called indirect costs of research, where the federal government covers a portion of the costs associated with funding projects, but this does not begin to cover the full cost of maintaining high-performance research activities.)

Over the past decade students and parents have been making rumbling noises—not as loudly as universities anticipated—about the relative decline in attention to student needs. Class sizes are growing. Teaching facilities are not keeping pace with research spaces (which are often supported with federal government funding that cannot be used for teaching purposes). Student support services and other quality of student-life initiatives seem to have been cut back. Yet tuition fees have jumped dramatically—nearly doubling in the past ten years (there are wide differences among provinces and programs, but Ontario's went from $3,300 to close to $6,000 per year for an arts degree)—and government grants have increased as well.

As long as the primary funding sources for universities remain tied to student enrolment this is not going to change. There are exceptions, including support for medical schools and other health-related activities. The College of Agriculture and Bioresources at the University of Saskatchewan, to single out a long-term success, has received direct funding for research from the provincial government for many years. But in general, governments have lumped all the base-budget and ongoing support for universities into a single grant, directly connected to the number of students in courses.

It's time for governments to provide a different funding model, one that provides a clearer and more direct indication of how they want universities to spend their money and effort. Funding research on the back of teaching essentially requires the universities to shift resources from the source of income to the area of expenditure. Students mistakenly think the government is supporting their learning activities when, in fact, the direct contribution to undergraduate instruction is actually quite limited. As things stand, the vast majority of provincial and federal government funding directed to universities goes into research.

Coming clean will be politically difficult. Governments like the status quo. Their message should read as follows:

> *We are providing University X with fifty million dollars. Of that funding, we expect them to spend forty million on research. We are pleased to fund sabbaticals, the 40 per cent of faculty members' time devoted to research, highly specialized research facilities and library holdings, conference attendance, and the hiring of research assistance in this manner and we truly believe that our communities, province, and country will be better off as a result. We are also providing University X with ten million dollars towards the cost of teaching, realizing that this represents only a small percentage of the total cost associated with this important activity. As a government, we believe that students, the prime beneficiaries of an undergraduate education, should pay the lion's share of the costs of their degree.*

Don't hold your breath. The traditional approach will likely continue.

Digital Technologies

A decade or so ago, when Conrad Black was in his ascendancy, newspapers and local radio stations were seen as a licence to print money, and the music industry seemed to have a hammerlock on kids' wallets. Then the digital revolution hit. Napster made copying music a snap. BitTorrent introduced file sharing to youth culture and transformed movie viewing from an evening at the theatre to a cozy snuggle with one's laptop. On-line newspapers, radio stations, blogs, discussion forums, and the like nibbled away at the information lifeblood of the news industry, and Kijiji and craigslist drove a stake through the want-ads, the heart of the newspapers' business models. What a change—and in such a short time.

Many people think that universities will be on the hit list soon. University education, particularly as practiced in Canada, is very old tech and very low tech. Classrooms might have projection capabilities and professors might put their notes on-line, but Canadian universities are only playing on the fringes of the digital revolution.

The warning signs are out there—the new technologies are transforming the way students learn and the way universities teach. In many countries, huge on-line universities, with 200,000 students or more, provide education to students through digital means.

What do the following institutions have in common: Alama Iqbal Open University (Pakistan), Indira Gandhi National Open University (India), Anadolu University (Turkey), Universitas Terbuka (Indonesia), Bangladesh Open University (Bangladesh)? First, they are all distance education/on-line universities (Anadolu has a traditional campus but the on-line section is by far the largest, enrolling more than 870,000 students). Second, they are all in the top ten largest universities in the world—Alama Iqbal has three million students; Bangladesh Open University has a mere 600,000 and is seventh largest.

Some North American public institutions are adapting to the new technologies. The Western Governors University, an on-line consortium of American schools, has more than 19,000 students. The largest digital university in the United States, the University of Phoenix On-line, has more than 220,000 students (or more than the University of Toronto, Alberta, British Columbia, and the University of Montreal combined) the largest conventional university in the States, Ohio State, has a mere 53,000 students (or fewer than the University of Toronto).

The biggest Canadian competitors—Athabasca University (38,000 students, most studying by distance education), the Open University of British Columbia/Thompson Rivers University, and Télé-Université Québec—are much smaller and serve targeted audiences. The Ontario government announced in 2010 a significant shift towards distance education/on-line learning, although it hasn't unveiled a formal plan yet.

On-line education, however, may only be the tip of the iceberg. Students' use of technology—from iPhones to BlackBerrys, instant messaging to Google—is well ahead of most instructors'. So too have their learning styles, attention spans, and understanding of expertise and knowledge been transformed by instant access to the Internet. Interactions with peers, now encouraged through seminars and discussion groups, will take place globally by video-conferencing devices, likely working through portable devices or home computers. Academic research—both the collection of data and the sharing of results and ideas—has yet to catch up with the possibilities of the new technologies—let alone the technologies coming down the line. The role of professors will likely change dramatically, as will learning styles.

In a decade or so, massive investments in physical classrooms, long-term commitments to tenure-stream faculty, and even the concept of the old-style residential campus could well seem archaic, or at best a luxury for the rich.

And further down the line, who knows? University degrees by intra-venous injection? What we do know is that major change is in the offing, student expectations are shifting dramatically, and great opportunities await the institutions and jurisdictions that first figure out the new way forward. Ironically, although university researchers played such a big role in the development of the Internet and new digital devices, universities appear to be well behind the curve in making the most of the digital age.

Accessibility Is Entrenching Academic Mediocrity

One of our colleagues is a poster child for accessibility. He had a rambunc-tious youth until maturity (and love) straightened him out. He got a late start in the academy, attending an open-entry community college. He followed his then-girlfriend to university, discovered a love of learning, and continued his studies. He improved every step of the way, getting rave reviews as a student, securing a faculty position, and succeeding admirably as a scholar. Without open entry, he would have been denied a university education; the country would have been denied a fine teacher and talented academic.

This story, and there are many like it, makes the following statement that much harder to write: governments' obsession with accessibility—a seat for all of those who wish to study—is undermining the quality of university education and entrenching mediocrity as a hallmark of the Canadian system.

A conversation between a Deputy Minister of Advanced Education and a university administrator several years back went something like this. The DM asked the administrator if it was possible to produce more graduates without an infusion of funds. He was told there was a way that would not cost anyone any money. The DM was thrilled and asked what could be done. The answer: refuse admission to the least qualified 25 per cent, but keep the university's funding the same. Improve the quality of the entering class, reduce class sizes, and give faculty and staff more time to deal with a smaller and more talented group of students.

Net result, said the administrator, was a guarantee of more graduates— with the lowest 40 per cent of the first-year class already failing to complete their degrees, the loss of the least able 25 per cent of the incoming class would not reduce graduating rates much. The DM turned pale, told the university administrator to keep the idea to himself and never revisited the topic. Why? Because ensuring that Mary and Johnny have access to university—where they could fail or succeed on their own—was the single most important political priority in the Canadian university system.

Since Canadian universities are funded primarily on the basis of enrolment, they have been reluctant to restrict admissions unless they are bursting at the seams. Queen's University, a fine Ontario school, opted not to expand enrolment during the early twenty-first century, and continues to pay a substantial financial price for the decision.

Institutions have a strong incentive to grow, even when the pool of students is small and, in some jurisdictions, declining significantly. So grade point averages for admission either stay low or decline, or are overcome by high school grade inflation. Students who are ill prepared or ill suited for university are admitted, only—in many cases—to drop out. Bright students in the classes can be resentful of the less talented and motivated among their number, and professors are discouraged by the poor skills of many of their students.

If Canadian institutions want to maintain and improve their academic standards, they would be well advised to start by raising the bar to admission and ensuring that incoming students have the skills to succeed. Consider this. The department chair of physics at a leading Japanese university was asked how many students they admitted every year. The number was 150. He was asked how many graduated. He looked puzzled. "I told you, 150." A similar conversation with a top university in Hong Kong produced the same reply: the number of students admitted was almost exactly the same as the number who graduated. Ask a comparable question to a Canadian institution, and prepare to be surprised—and dismayed—by the answer.

The story is not all bad. Alberta and British Columbia have it right. They offer open-entry colleges and teaching universities for students unable to secure a place in a research university. These institutions—places like Mount Royal and Grant McEwan in Alberta, Vancouver Island University, Capilano University, and University of the Fraser Valley in British Columbia—do a very fine job teaching students of varying academic backgrounds. Students eager and able to move to a larger university can do so, typically after the first or second year. Others complete their studies in the teaching institution and then proceed to successful graduate and professional careers.

All high school students should have the opportunity to continue their studies and to capitalize on their intellectual potential and determination. But they should not have the right to go to any institution they want to. It should be difficult to get into a top university, and it should mean something to be accepted. Open access undercuts the intellectual and competitive challenge of getting into university. Just compare the efforts of lackadaisical Canadian students in the last year of high school to those facing oppressive national examinations in Japan, China, Hong Kong, and other nations—or compare it with Canadian students of fifty years go. If Asia goes too far in one direction, Canada has gone too far in the other. Give students alternate routes to a university degree, and allow them to proceed on the basis of accomplishment—not what they or their parents think they deserve.

95 Universities Need International Students

In 2010 the Government of Ontario told its universities and the general public that it wanted to double the number of international students in the coming years. The Government of Canada has made a similar commitment, providing national funding for an international recruiting effort. Universities, big and small, are chasing applicants from around the world. There is a great deal at stake here, including the long-term viability of some Canadian universities.

International students provide a welcome boost to the economy, both in their tuition fees and in the money they spend on living expenses—usually substantially more than the fees. Australia, which has devoted enormous energy to this area in recent years, identifies international student education as its third-largest export. Post-secondary education is drawing billions of dollars in foreign income a year into the national economy—and it's a cleaner export than coal. That's why governments are enthusiastic about international student recruitment, both in helping to pay for universities and for bringing in offshore money generally.

The financial logic of international student recruitment is easy to follow. International students do not get government grants, except in Nova Scotia and (some students) in Quebec, where the province has identified international students as a growth sector for the economy and as a means of attracting immigrants. But they do pay high tuition fees—in most cases two to three times the rate for domestic students. Attracting international students can be a financial bonanza because the extra teaching costs of adding one or two students to already large classes are small. The truth is that now, they're more commonly a way of bailing out the institution.

In the real world the numbers don't work out quite so favourably. It costs money to recruit international students—historically more than $1,000 per confirmed student. The students require additional support and assistance, particularly relating to English language skills and cultural adaptation. Many of the students struggle academically, for complex reasons related to language, the stresses associated with being in a foreign country, and unevenness in academic preparation. As universities become more dependent upon foreign-student revenue they often lower their English language requirements and offer students a chance to pick up basic skills in introductory and preparatory courses. A significant number of the students arrive as international students, apply for landed-immigrant status, gain the new standing, and switch to a lower domestic fee before they graduate. As a consequence, the profits from 100 incoming international students dwindle substantially through academic attrition and changing immigration status.

Another problem is that international students also tend not to distribute themselves evenly among the academic disciplines. Few students from Pakistan or China come to this country to study Northern Canadian history or to explore modern philosophy. They come, in the main, for very practical reasons, seeking an English language credential that will secure them a job, either in Canada or in their home country. As a result, they tend to cluster in certain areas—like business-related fields, engineering, science, and technology. They tend to stay away from the social sciences, humanities, and health areas. And as international students become a big part of the student population the shift towards these applied and practical areas will increase.

Canadians are ambivalent about international students. While there is official acceptance of the argument that bringing international students to the country will generate more highly skilled workers, many Canadians worry that the newcomers are displacing Canadians seeking to get into the best programs. In November 2010 the Ontario government announced a thirty-million-dollar program (two-thirds from government, one-third from the universities) to attract seventy-five of the top graduate students in the world to the province's graduate programs—offering them each $40,000 a year to come. (Quebec has an even better deal, but only for francophone students: they get fast-track approval for permanent residency in Canada). While the universities celebrated the investment in world-class talent, opposition leader Tim Hudak had a different view: "This is just another example of how Dalton McGuinty's priorities are out of touch with those of average families..." he said. "When families in Ontario today can't afford their kids to go to college or university without piling up huge debts, to give $40,000 a year to foreign students? That's just wrong."

International students enrich and enliven universities. They bring new perspectives, experiences, and ideas to the academic mix. But our growing financial dependence on international students carries significant risks. International students are, in effect, propping up and improving universities for all in attendance. If they stop coming, the universities will feel financial pain.

96 Some of Our Best Grads Are Leaving

Where do students want to go when they graduate? When Ontario students are polled (unscientifically, we should add) most say they expect to stay in Ontario, but some say they would seriously consider relocating to the United States. At least a quarter declare an openness to head to Europe or Asia. A much smaller group—perhaps 15 per cent—are open to BC or Alberta. Ask about Saskatchewan and the Maritimes and the students roll their eyes. Ah, Ontario…

There's a worrisome message here for Canadians. A sizable number of university students are willing—some are even eager—to leave the country upon graduation. They don't seem to need huge incentives to leave: the prospect of finding a job more easily, getting a slightly higher salary, and living in a warmer place seem to be enough to get them looking beyond the borders.

It is not that Canadian university students are leaving the country in droves, like educated rats leaving a sinking ship. Most will in fact stay, many in their province of education. International students and new Canadians often return to their country of origin, a fairly logical part of the life cycle but accelerating due to the economic rise of China and India.

The problem rests not with the average graduate, but with the departure of key people, either those with entrepreneurial drive or highly specialized skills. Companies often need employees with very specific training, so the loss of these people can make it difficult for local firms to operate. These, of course, are precisely the graduates most likely to leave, to chase the greater venture capital pots or higher-paying, exciting jobs in other places. Some of the key graduates from Canada's universities—the number and percentage remain uncertain—may be lost soon after they finish their studies.

Saskatchewan has tried to deal with the issue by instituting a Graduate Retention Program that provides a rebate of up to $20,000 for university graduates who have graduated from a provincial institution and who live and pay income taxes in the province. It has recently been expanded to include graduates from outside the province (and outside Canada) who move to the province and work there.

There's an interesting twist to this issue. When students at a large gathering were challenged as to why they were so willing to leave and—as a provocation to challenge them—so disloyal to the country that had supported them so well, they sat soberly. One student put up his hand: "Well sir, no one ever asked me to stay." So we must ask them to stay. We need the best and brightest to stay here, unless our long-term plan is either that of the Maritimes—sending the graduates "down the road"—or the Philippines, hoping that the overseas workers will send remittances back home to keep the country afloat. Neither option is good for Canada.

97 Struggling with English

A professional friend runs a major high-tech company that hires hundreds of people each year. He has one rule, set in stone: if they can't write effectively, don't hire them. It's very simple: if their English skills aren't sufficient, they won't succeed in the company.

This policy makes sense. Studies have shown that writing ability is one of the single most important determinants of career success. Even in a high-tech, science-based world, where specialized skills are vital to personal and organizational achievement, the capacity to write effectively is hugely important. Add to this the ability to read and make effective presentations and a core truism of the modern world stands out: English language ability is critical.

This crucial observation should make universities very nervous, for their attention to writing skills can be haphazard, and is often not up to the requirements of the workforce. There is unevenness on campus. Writing expectations are higher in the arts than in the sciences. Students with English as a second language—international and domestic—have more difficulties than native English speakers. On the whole, however, universities do not do enough to test and improve English language skills.

It's not for want of trying. Schools have tried entrance examinations (although the bar for success is not very high). They offer remedial writing assistance and workshops for students with difficulties. Some universities have instituted writing across the curriculum requirements to ensure that all students get exposure to writing assignments tied to their field of study. Many programs have gatekeeper courses that require substantial writing assignments.

But students can generally avoid such requirements if they want to. The student grapevine and ratemyprofessors.com identify professors who mark for grammar and test with written questions—and those who go easy on errors in presentation and set multiple-choice exams. Students with English language challenges can pay to have someone review their major papers. They can, if they really try, get around many of the language barriers.

The end result: a degree does not always mean the recipient can write and communicate effectively in English. This should be a central and obvious guarantee of a Canadian university education, but it is not. We can't say for sure how many students emerge with serious deficiencies in this regard. An educated guess—and it is only a guess—is that some 20 per cent of graduates likely have career-limiting writing deficiencies. This is too high. A *quarter* of this rate would be much too high. Universities must adopt measures to ensure that all graduates can work effectively and easily in English.

Canada Needs a Harvard

Or a Swarthmore, a Duke, a Princeton, a Yale, an MIT. You might say, who cares? Those places are expensive elitist institutions, and this is a book about Canada, where all universities are equal, because all Canadians are supposed to be equal. We could cite Japanese and Chinese examples to make the same point—Todai/Tokyo, Osaka, Tohoku, Fudan, National Taiwan University—but the American ones are more familiar to us.

American, Japanese, and Chinese universities are clearly not all equal, and Yale, Princeton, MIT, and a dozen other top private institutions in those countries set the world standard for research-intensive universities. Flush with endowments, freed from government intervention, they are the best of the best. They stockpile Nobel Prize winners, attract the best graduate students, influence governments, and set global agendas. Much the same is true at the undergraduate level, where Swarthmore, Middlebury, Reed, Gettysburg, Grinnell, and similar elite private colleges provide an unparalleled quality of university education. But you have to be very rich or very intelligent to get into them.

Canada's elite research institutions want to play in the big international leagues, and some of them do, but they are hamstrung by the fact that they are all public institutions that charge much lower fees than their American counterparts. Dependent on government money they must operate on smaller budgets, and they must do as the government tells them. MIT has a student-faculty ratio of 9 to 1; Waterloo, which compares itself to the elite Boston institution, has a ratio of 26 to 1. Harvard's endowment is more than $36 billion, even after the market meltdown. Toronto, with three times as many students as Harvard, has an endowment of $1.4 billion, down from $1.75 billion in 2008. Put another way, Harvard's endowment per student is 100 times greater than Toronto's. Toronto does well by world standards, but it is no Harvard, and much of the difference depends on money. Yale spends more than $120,000 per student, although much less is actually devoted to their needs.

The situation is worse at the smaller, liberal arts colleges. Our best small schools—Acadia, St. Francis Xavier, Mount Alison, and Bishop's—are poverty-stricken compared to their American counterparts. Swarthmore, with only 1,800 students, has an endowment ($1.5 billion) that beats the University of Toronto. Colorado College has more than $400 million in the bank and uses the money to provide its students with an outstanding educational experience. Canadian schools do their best with what they have, but what they have is not enough to compete with the Americans.

They cannot match the facilities, educational experience, and social life of the elite American private colleges and universities. In financial terms, Canada is stuck on a single, government-funded model of university operations. True, not all private American institutions are rich. Some have closed in the past few years and others have partnered with for-profit on-line education providers to keep the doors open. But if private institutions of the Harvard type can be so impressive, why has Canada shunned this model? The answer is simply that this is not the Canadian way of doing things, and the situation is unlikely to change.

Why? For one thing, no philanthropist has stepped forward with a large enough donation to pay for a truly serious attempt. When King Abdullah University of Science and Technology opened in Saudi Arabia in 2009 it had a $10 billion endowment, with minimal government control. No Canadian billionaire is able or willing to put up that kind of money. The basic problem is that Canadians expect government to provide university education for everyone, and cheaply. Private schools seem anti-Canadian, catering to the wealthy, undermining our commitment to the common good. Even the wealthy want the public to pay for their children's university costs. Canadians who are willing and able to pay for the best, or who want the prestige of an Ivy League degree, go to the United States. Canada gets to remain virtuous, sticking with the public university model, because the option of private education is open south of the border.

If private universities in the United States set the gold standard—and they do—then Canada has chosen the silver, or perhaps the bronze. Canadian institutions provide some of the best value for money in the world, working efficiently and effectively in education and research. But the growing network of world-class research and liberal arts institutions either has access to massive amounts of private funding or generous government support. Our universities have neither, and the results of our funding model are beginning to show.

It's not hard to imagine a successful Canadian private institution, probably an elite undergraduate school. The model and even the opportunity exist, but the prospect remains dim. Private university education is—to use the ultimate horror phrase of the political left in this country—an "American-style" system, and anathema to a majority of Canadians.

99 Top Priority: Teaching and Learning

The Canadian university system is based, almost entirely, on a forty-year-old model of post-secondary education whose roots go back much further. Universities were places where faculty members did research and taught and, if the institutions were large enough, worked at both the undergraduate and graduate levels. All faculty members were expected to be active in research, although expectations and results varied a fair bit between Nowhere U and the University of Toronto. That model worked when 10 to 15 per cent of students attended university. It doesn't work so well now that a much larger proportion of high school graduates go to university.

Canada desperately needs a network of high-quality universities that put teaching first. British Columbia has figured this out, developing an extensive system of community colleges that offer first- and second-year university courses, later transforming some of them into university colleges and now universities. The mandates for these new institutions—Capilano, Fraser Valley, Kwantlen, Thompson Rivers, and Vancouver Island—explicitly restrict research activity, although all of the campuses have some very capable and accomplished scholars. Much the same is true for Grant McEwan University and Mount Royal University in Alberta, where teaching clearly takes priority over research in the list of faculty responsibilities. A recent report in Ontario recommended a similar development. Quebec has this system, in part through the CEGEP system, which provides first-year university-level instruction in non-research environments.

We can be sure that faculty will resist a change to teaching-first institutions. The new institutions in BC and Alberta are facing pressure to become more like traditional universities. It's important that their mandates be clearly spelled out: PhD-qualified faculty where appropriate, faculty evaluation based on teaching achievements, substantially higher teaching loads (possibly including three-term teaching), library collections and laboratories based on undergraduate needs, and a strong focus on remedial assistance and campus life.

Institutions of this sort would teach more students and would operate more efficiently. They would emphasize student academic success, grounded in basic skills and comprehensive academic degrees. These universities would, by their very nature, be more applied, offering career-ready preparation. They would pay little attention to academic graduate degrees (students with aptitude and motivation could transfer after a year or two at the teaching-first university). The space currently allocated to research laboratories could be used for student social space. And faculty members would be expected to be readily available to meet with students and to assist with personal development and academic growth.

The shift away from the idea there is only one model for institutional success will not be an easy process, for many colleges wish to become universities, and teaching universities wish to become prestigious research universities. The cities are often part of the problem, for they want "real" universities, with all the bells and whistles and the status that attaches to graduate programs and research grants. UNBC, centred in Prince George, came into existence largely just for that reason—because the community rejected the idea of a teaching-first institution. Faculty members with PhDs want to be part of "real" universities too. There was rejoicing in Nanaimo, both on and off campus, when Malaspina College began to offer degrees as Malaspina University-College, and then as Vancouver Island University.

But to put it bluntly, Canada cannot possibly meet the demands for mass university education based on the model currently almost uniform across the country. If the conceit continues that half or more of all Canadian high school students are ready for, and capable of, completing a university degree, then cost-effective, student-focused, and substantially remedial institutions will be required. We must offer a caveat: degrees from teaching-first institutions generally carry less status than those from research universities—compare assumptions about the value of a degree from Southeast Missouri State University to one from Duke or the University of Michigan. In fairly short order, however, institutions earn a reputation based on the abilities and accomplishments of their graduates.

 # National Innovation

How are we are doing as a nation? One way to examine that question revolves around the "innovation equation": Education + Basic Research + Commercialization = Competitiveness and Prosperity.

In other words, if we ensure that students have a solid, advanced education, fund basic research at international competitive levels, and invest in the commercialization of new ideas, then presto! The country will be globally competitive, producing the wealth, jobs, and opportunity that will fuel twenty-first century competitiveness. It's a compelling line of argument, and it's being followed in countries around the world. Canadian universities have been pushing it for twenty years, and have convinced governments across the country to buy into the idea, leading to massive expansion in participation rates, well-funded basic research, and strong support for commercialization.

So without getting too technical, let's look at Canada's performance in terms of this equation. In general, the input factors in this country are favourable. Perhaps surprisingly, given the unkind things we've said about high school standards, it turns out that our students do quite well on high school tests. Global comparisons of math, reading, and science skills produce results that should make Canadians proud. The data fly almost directly in the face of our experience with first-year undergraduates.

Who would have guessed that, according to the Organisation for Economic Co-operation and Development, Canada is in third place in science, behind only Finland (a country that's getting a great deal right these days) and Hong Kong? (The United States was twenty-ninth.) Canada ranked seventh in the 2006 mathematics rankings, far ahead of the United States at thirty-fifth. We scored below Taipei, Finland, Hong Kong, South Korea, Netherlands, and Switzerland, but for a country that wallows in self-criticism and self-doubt, seventh place is no mean feat. In reading—and here is a real shocker given our experience with Canadian university students—Canadian fifteen-year-olds finished fourth behind South Korea, Finland, and Hong Kong. Nevertheless, the country's overall high school graduation rate of less than 80 per cent is well behind the leading nations—in this case Germany, Ireland, Japan, Finland, Korea, Greece, Norway, and the UK—all of which see more than 90 per cent of their students complete high school.

Our national research performance is also quite impressive. Our top universities do extremely well. In the *Times Higher Education Supplement* rankings Canada had nine universities in the top 200 for 2010–11: Toronto (17), UBC (30), McGill (35), McMaster (93), Alberta (127), Victoria (130), Montreal (138), Dalhousie (193), and Simon Fraser (199). According to the *Academic Ranking of World Universities*—an assessment of research output and impact—we lag behind the elite U.S. universities, but still place well globally: Toronto (27), UBC (36), McGill (61), McMaster (88), with Alberta and Montreal in the 101 to 150 band and Calgary and Waterloo in the next 50. Dalhousie, Laval, Queen's, Simon Fraser, Western Ontario, Guelph, Manitoba, Ottawa, Saskatchewan, and Victoria are ranked between 151 and 200 internationally. Drop down a notch to the 401 to 500 band of universities globally and Canada gets to add Carleton, Concordia, Quebec, Sherbrooke, and York. Twenty-three universities in the top 500 is no mean achievement. The United States, with ten times our population, has 154 in the top 500, the UK has thirty-eight, Japan only twenty-five, and

China a mere twenty-two (but come back in a decade and this will change dramatically).

The other critical input factor, total funding for research, is less impressive. Canada ranked only thirteenth in the OECD in 2007, spending less than 1.9 per cent of GDP on research activity (compared to an impressive 4.7 per cent for Israel and 3.5 for Sweden, Finland, and Japan). Interestingly, the Canadian percentage of expenditures on research by higher education institutions and government—more than 41 per cent—is the highest in the OCED. But expenditures by business on research represent the lowest percentage in this important comparison group. In total, for 2008, fully $10.3 billion of Canada's $29.5 billion of spending on R&D funnelled through universities, including more than $1 billion from the provincial governments and $2.75 billion from the government of Canada. The problem, it appears, is not a shortage of government investment in research but rather under-investment by Canadian business. Governments have also made substantial investments in commercialization initiatives, funding technology transfer offices and other supports for new companies.

In terms of human capital and financial investment in post-secondary education, then, Canada does very well. We produce globally competitive students from our high schools (and to answer the nagging question, Canadian research on the results of the surveys of fifteen-year-olds shows that the top-ranked students do very well in university). We send a very high percentage of our high school graduates to university and to college. The universities themselves are well funded, and governments are strongly supportive of academic research. University faculty members are also well paid: Canada has the highest entering salaries for new faculty members—ranking second only to Saudi Arabia in overall salaries—paying 2.2 times the national GDP per faculty member. On those elements controlled by governments, Canada does well by its university system.

Yet despite being highly competitive—if not a world leader—on the input side of the "innovation equation," on the output side, Canada is lagging behind. The commercialization of science falls well behind other nations, and there is concern about Canada's ability to keep up in the new economy. Our contributions in key areas—patents, commercialized products, and economic growth related to academic work—fall well behind our competitors. Check out Israel if you want to see a country getting this innovation package right, and look at what South Korea, Finland, and Taiwan have been doing lately.

The Conference Board of Canada examined this issue in 2010 and produced a worrying result. Canada ranked fourteenth out of the seventeen countries surveyed, and received a rating of "D" for our national effort. Switzerland topped the charts with a grade "A," followed by three "B" grades—Ireland, Japan, and the United States.

Overall, this is a mixed message. Canada has bought into the innovation equation, and governments have provided impressive support. But the corporate sector has not done its share, and this clearly hurts. What's more, the transition from investment in post-secondary education to true and sustained innovation output has fallen well short of national and regional aspirations. We are not well situated to be truly competitive in the twenty-first century economy and are not keeping up with key competitors. But the universities are not at fault. Funded to train more students, produce more graduates, produce more basic research, and support commercialization initiatives, Canadian institutions have responded.

We believe that the innovation equation needs to be rethought. Other variables—entrepreneurial culture, loyalty to the country, consumer environments, and national spirit—need to be considered. Universities have benefited enormously from government commitment to the innovation equation. Even if it is not in their collective interest to do so, they need to rethink their role in national innovation and work with governments, business, and the public to develop a Canadian strategy for prosperity.

For twenty years, Canada's universities have benefited from a belief that investment in students, graduate programs, basic research, and commercialization would build our new economy. The model does not appear to be working. Universities are clearly important, but not in their current role and format. We need to reinvent this role and, in the process, give Canada a real shot at twenty-first century prosperity.

Epilogue: Preparing Canada's Universities for the Challenges Ahead

Let's be realistic. Not all universities are going to survive the next fifty years. The problems are serious, and the university and college system in Canada faces unprecedented pressures in the distribution of students, government funding, rising costs, public and parental expectations, contribution to economic development, and particularly, accessibility and the capacity to address national and regional social concerns. There will never be enough money to meet these demands and expectations.

How can our institutions best ensure they will be winners and not losers in 2060? There are many important things they can and must do to anticipate and respond to changing conditions. And so—boldly sticking our necks out and charging recklessly into the unknown—we offer the following recommendations for Canadian universities:

High quality is the number one assurance of success. Top quality institutions, faculties, departments, and faculty members flourish. Mediocrity—which is in danger of becoming Canada's national mantra—is a death sentence. In the coming years institutions that stick to low standards will become like high schools; institutions that commit themselves to pre-eminence in some or all fields will prosper. Universities should drop the language of "excellence," and aspire to be the best. Being the best does not mean emulating the major research universities. A university that is the best at teaching poorly prepared students will be successful in the long-term.

Be future makers, not future takers. Passivity in the face of change is a death sentence. Creative and positive response—knowing that there will be failures and stumbles along the way—is essential. Universities should establish an "Institutional Future Committee," charged with monitoring social, economic, political, and cultural affairs on a national and global basis and proposing detailed responses to the university community. This committee should be one of the most prominent on campus. Universities are research institutions. They should—and do—understand the contextual forces shaping our world better than anyone. This ability has to be harnessed, and attended to, by the institutions themselves.

Specialization works. Canada, we have already argued, has dozens of universities but really only one model for how universities operate, despite the fact that there have always been possibilities to break out of the mould. We need the courage to be different in this country, to avoid replicating our major universities on a regional or local basis. Universities need to decide what they do best and what they do differently. And they need to allow this difference to permeate the institution. This takes courage and determination—and a willingness to be different.

Universities need to understand better the differences in the student population. We argued that students generally fit into one of three streams. They are either at university for remedial assistance, career preparation, or academic and professional development. Universities need to decide where their focus will be and/or develop programs that meet the needs of two or three groups. Each institution should determine its priorities and preferred approaches. The system should stop, however, assuming that one set of programs and courses will adequately meet the needs of all students. A few smaller universities should turn themselves into elite liberal arts and sciences institutions, along American models.

It's time to institutionalize the two-tier faculty system already in place. Canadian egalitarianism, and an unwillingness to call a spade a spade, have compelled us to pretend that everyone is both a researcher and teacher. We now, in addition, have a vast army of contract, sessional, and part-time faculty members who desperately want stability, recognition, and a chance at a full career. We must do away with the research requirement for these faculty without designating them as second-class, and in return require them to teach more. The creation of two-tier faculty arrangements—essentially continuing lecturer positions for teaching-intensive faculty members and research and teaching tenure-track positions—will recognize the current reality, provide protection and security for a cadre of excellent and deserving university teachers, while acknowledging the real needs of the university environment.

Career readiness should be a key policy of the modern university system. People expect universities to produce career-ready graduates, and the students themselves are at the forefront of this demand. Universities can maintain many of their programs and courses as at present, but they need to expand career-preparation programs for undergraduates, add professional Master's programs for graduates, develop new and more intense ties with employers, and adjust some of what they do to ensure that graduates are, indeed, heading into the workforce fully prepared and ready for exciting and dynamic careers.

Colleges and universities need to integrate their offerings in creative and mutually beneficial ways. The old distinctions do no one any good— it's high time colleges and universities began to co-operate. Coordinated offerings—including arrangements where students enroll in both college and university at the same time and, perhaps, complete both a college diploma and a university degree in a five-year period—should become commonplace. The academically elite institutions are, however, unlikely to go far down this path. The locally focused institutions should take a close look at models like Nipissing University and Canadore College, two institutions that share a common footprint in North Bay.

Tenure has to go—or at least it has to change. Academic freedom and job security are two very different considerations and must be separated. Academic freedom must be ensured, and indeed university faculty should be speaking out much more than they currently do. But universities must have the ability to reassign resources and faculty positions to areas of need and away from areas of declining demand. Without such a change—easily the hardest thing to do in a university setting—in a decade or two some universities will make General Motors look like a fast-moving start-up company.

Universities have to move quickly into the digital age. And they can start by requiring all students and faculty to participate in on-line courses. Universities should require all students to take a minimum of one course per semester on-line. They should also require that all faculty put one or more courses on-line. This is no longer an optional exercise, but rather an integral part of how people study, learn, teach, and communicate. More to the point, on-line learning will evolve rapidly along with new technologies—universities have to have their finger in the clay in order to play an effective role in designing the educational future.

Student choice in first- and second-year course offerings should be scaled back. Sorry to sound Paleolithic, but universities know what students need to learn better than the students do. It's vital that students be given more direction, as happens in engineering and some science and professional programs. Getting agreement will be difficult, but if university faculty cannot define what a foundation year or two should be, then there is something wrong with their approach to education.

Competency-based learning is essential. Universities need to define, program by program, what skills are required of graduates. These skills should then be tied to specified mandatory courses. Students who do not develop appropriate skills in all compulsory areas should not progress or graduate. It is just as important that an arts graduate be numerate as it is that an engineering graduate be able to write. A university degree has to mean something clear and irrefutable. It used to, but currently it does not.

The approach to the education of international students has to change dramatically. Students from other countries need to be provided with what they are seeking—a high-quality education in an English-speaking environment. Universities need to shift away from an emphasis in recruiting based on entrance standards to a combination of academic potential and exit standards (defining what students need to know in order to get a degree). Most international students need degree-long assistance with English as a second language. New approaches and an emphasis on exit standards could result in major improvements in the educational experience for foreign students.

Universities need to lead the digital revolution. Universities in this country, working collaboratively with government and the private sector, should be at the forefront of the digital revolution. Libraries have done a superb job of putting materials on-line, but student and faculty receptiveness needs to be greatly improved. Bookstores are seriously out of date in this regard but could be at the vanguard of bringing e-books into this country. E-seminars could be effectively integrated into the undergraduate and graduate experience, just as e-lectures could expand the reach and impact of faculty experience. The future of digital media likely rests with ubiquitous computing. University environments are almost ideal testing grounds for this kind of revolutionary technology. University researchers provide a great deal of the digital innovation that is changing the world. Oddly, universities are very slow adopters. This has to change.

Universities need more revenue streams. It's time to consider radical alternatives to traditional sources of funding. Why not buy a gas station and promote its use to students, faculty, staff, alumni, and community supporters? Some universities—Queen's, Western, Alberta, and UBC—could capitalize on their brand recognition and do as the big American universities do—earn income off residuals (how many sweatshirts do you have to sell to pay a faculty member's salary?). Some universities own land and develop commercial housing. One, Guelph, runs a commercial gravel pit. Others lease out residence space for conferences. Very few have commercial consulting practices that capitalize on faculty skills (and on the abilities of academic spouses—one of the greatest untapped sources of expertise in the country). Something along these lines needs to be done. Government grants will likely continue to decline. Resistance to tuition increases will continue. Donations will remain targeted at special projects. All costs will rise. Without additional revenue streams universities will likely find themselves in a steadily accelerating fiscal nightmare in the years to come.

Universities need to rediscover their universality. Universities need to determine the key elements of a learned society that must be imparted to all students. All students need to understand the rudiments of science, mathematics, language, culture, history, and philosophy. They need to know the key thinkers in each of the disciplines, and need to know where the frontiers of learning are in all subject areas. They need to be globally aware and internationally prepared. In terms of the education of the undergraduate, narrowness of focus can produce narrowness of mind. Universities must stand for comprehensive understanding, even if it means cutting back on some elements of disciplinary training.

Universities need to collaborate to capitalize on administrative efficiencies. There are some terrific examples already in existence. The Canadian Association of Research Libraries has revolutionized digital-information sharing. Universities collaborate on insurance, through a national shared-insurance system, saving millions of dollars in annual premiums. The centralized Ontario and British Columbia application centres have cut costs dramatically in this increasingly important area. There are local examples, like the tri-university library consortium between the University of Waterloo, the University of Guelph, and Wilfrid Laurier University. The collaboration among the University of New Brunswick (Fredericton), the University of New Brunswick (Saint John), and including St. Thomas University is in many respects a model of collegiality, co-operation, and good sense. Many more opportunities like this are often lost behind institutional priorities.

Universities need to redefine their expectations of faculty members. Traditional models of academic engagement—scholarly articles, academic books, research grants, and conference papers are all fine activities and should be continued and rewarded. But academics who help draft a new law, support an advocacy group, tackle a pressing social problem, work with a community, explain scientific matters to children in school, or otherwise apply their scholarly knowledge and professional abilities in an appropriate manner should also be recognized for doing so. Incentives matter and rarely more intensely than in the university setting.

The scholarship of synthesis must be elevated to the highest level of respect and credibility. Keeping up with the Everest of literature in any field is almost impossible or, to put it more accurately, is possible only by defining the field in increasingly narrow terms. The generalist, the scholar who can make sense of the material, find connections and dissonance, and bring order to the scholarly enterprise, will be a key figure in twenty-first century academia. Universities need to recognize that the ability to synthesize learning—equal to, if not above the ability to conduct original research—is essential if we are to survive the massive wave of scholarly writing and find the most important lessons and insights in the wealth of original studies.

Universities should lead, not resist, the revolution in course and program design. Wiki architecture—enabling scholars from around the world to contribute to the development of course material—will forever change the way we assemble course material and teach. Courses placed on the web and available for regular revision and editorial change will be available in many languages (thanks to rapidly improving web-based translation devices) and could be listened to by students (check out the vocal abilities of the latest Kindle e-book). Faculty from different backgrounds, cultures, experiences, and value systems can collaborate to create, maintain, and adapt courses—and retain their individuality through the actual delivery of the course on-line or in person. It really is time to get with the current generation.

Universities need to update and rationalize their governance systems. Governance reform is essential. Certain key elements will have to be maintained—faculty control over academic programs, and board control over financial and administrative matters. But streamlining, technology-based solutions, limitation of mandates, and other considerations must be taken into account. New financial realities will require greater attention to the speed of decision-making, flexibility in resource allocations, the capacity to open and close programs more quickly, responsiveness to societal and economic trends, and a much higher level of innovation. Governance systems will have to be amended to respond to these realities.

Universities must stop trying (and pretending) to be all alike. At the risk of repeating this fact once too often, we will say it one final time. We must abandon the "Lake Wobegon" model, in which all places are above average, and all pretend to be high-quality research and teaching institutions. This pretense, which was never true and is becoming increasingly more untrue, is a recipe for mediocrity, decline, and ultimate disaster. Instead, different institutions should adopt different models, aiming for different markets and different goals. Canada supposedly celebrates diversity, and must do so in our post-secondary system. The sooner the better.

The Canadian university system is not in crisis—yet. But even those who love the institution, and count us foremost among them, know that substantial change is in the offing. Universities cannot be sacred cows— they take too much public and private money to maintain their aloofness and isolation. There are many good ideas and even better opportunities. Hanging onto the status quo is just about the worst thing for these vital institutions to do.

Sources

A wealth of information on Canadian and foreign universities is available to anyone with access to a computer. All universities have websites, where information about enrolment size, courses offered, fees, calendars, and the like can be found. The Canadian Association of University Teachers, Statistics Canada, the Canadian Federation of Students, and Provincial Departments of Post-Secondary Education are all good sources of information, as is *The Chronicle of Higher Education,* an American publication that publishes superb articles on post-secondary education that are relevant to Canada as well. The figures on participation rates for men and women in post-secondary education cited throughout this book come from Statistics Canada. Among the most useful sources for information on Canadian Universities are the Bulletin of the Canadian Association of University Teachers (available on-line), *University Affairs,* and the "Rae Report" (a 2005 review of post-secondary education in Ontario chaired by former premier Bob Rae). The annual *Maclean's* university issue is invaluable, as is a similar annual report from the Toronto *Globe and Mail.*

Books worth reading on Canadian universities include *Academic Transformation: Forces Reshaping Higher Education in Ontario* by Ian D. Clark, Greg Moran, Michael L. Skolnik, and David Trick, McGill-Queen's University Press, 2009; Robert Bothwell, David Bercuson, and J.L. Granatstein, *The Great Brain Robbery,* Toronto: McClelland and Stewart, 1984; Robert Bothwell, *Petrified Campus: the Crisis in Canada's Universities,* Toronto: Random House, 1998; James Cote and Anton L. Allahar, *Ivory Tower Blues: A University System in Crisis,* Toronto: University of Toronto Press, 2007; James L. Turk, ed., *Universities at Risk: How Politics, Special Interests and Corporatization Threaten Academic Integrity,* Toronto: Lorimer, 2008; Howard C. Clark, *Growth and Governance of Canadian Universities: An Insider's View,* Vancouver: UBC Press, 2003; Tom Pocklington and Allan Tupper, *No Place to Learn: Why Universities Aren't Working,* Vancouver: UBC Press, 2002; and Indhu Rajagopal, *Hidden Academics: Contract Faculty in Canadian Universities,* Toronto: University of Toronto Press, 2002.

There are far more books per capita on American universities than on

Canadian ones, a fact reflecting the struggle to get into the best universities and the equally intense battle to succeed academically in the less prestigious, open-entry campuses. The United States has a large number of the world's best and wealthiest universities, and a much larger number struggling to cope with the same financial, student, and faculty issues that we have described for Canada. A partial listing of recent books published in the past two years alone provides some indication of the American obsession with their universities: Jonathan R. Cole, *The Great American University: Its Rise to Preeminence, Its Indispensable National Role, Why It Must Be Protected*; Gaye Tuchman, *Wannabe U: Inside the Corporate University*; Derek Curtis Bok, *Universities in the Marketplace: The Commercialization of Higher Education*; Mark C. Taylor, *Crisis on Campus: A Bold Plan for Reforming Our Colleges and Universities*; Frank Donoghue, *The Last Professors: The Corporate University and the Fate of the Humanities*; Marc Bousquet and Cary Nelson, *How the University Works: Higher Education and the Low-Wage Nation*; Louis Menand, *The Marketplace of Ideas: Reform and Resistance in the American University*; Ben Wildavsky, *The Great Brain Race: How Global Universities Are Reshaping the World*; Holden Thorp and Buck Goldstein, *Engines of Innovation: The Entrepreneurial University in the Twenty-First Century*; David Horowitz, *Reforming Our Universities: The Campaign For An Academic Bill Of Rights*; William G. Bowen et al., *Crossing the Finish Line: Completing College at America's Public Universities*; Taylor Walsh and William G. Bowen, *Unlocking the Gates: How and Why Leading Universities Are Opening Up Access to Their Courses*.

Chapter 1

"The drop-out rate." Sometimes this means the number of first-year students who don't come back for a second year, and sometimes it means students who don't complete a degree. In 2006 Concordia University reported that only 54 per cent of its full-time students completed a degree in six years (*Vancouver Sun*, October 31, 2006). At the University of Windsor in 2010, 20 per cent of first-year students did not return for a second year. (CTV News on-line, November 3, 2010. See also *Edmonton Journal*, November 21, 2007). The figure of 92 per cent comes from McGill Enrolment Services Admissions Profile, Fall 2009 Admissions, http://www.mcgill.ca/es/profile.

Chapter 4

Historical statistics on tuition fees and student debt levels are available on-line from Statistics Canada. Current fees are posted on each university's website.

Chapter 6

Macleans.ca on campus, February 26, 2008, has a discussion of the victory lap, with particularly interesting comments from students. See also Kelly Pedro, "The Victory Lap," London *Free Press*, August 29, 2009 on-line. Forty-five per cent of Ontario students do not complete high school in four years.

Chapter 7

The McGill News Alumni Quarterly for Fall 1998 has a good article on the admission process, written in the days when the cut-off rate was 80 per cent.

Chapter 10

Figures for participation by age and gender are taken, here and elsewhere in this book, from Statistics Canada. Rick Miner's book is available on-line. The figures for the number of high school graduates in Ontario can be found at http://www.edu.gov.on.ca/eng/teachers/studentsuccess/CCL_SSE_Report.pdf, and the number from that province accepting offers of admission to universities at http://www.ouac.on.ca/statistics/ugrad-con-stats/ucon_september.

Chapter 11

The figure on graduates working at jobs for which they are overqualified comes from "Where do graduates end up doing unskilled work? And earning most?" *The Economist*, September 9, 2010.

Chapter 17

Rae's call for higher fees, along with increased grants, was not well received by the Canadian Federation of Students. See vivelecanada.ca, February 7, 2005.

Chapter 20

The Japanese are worried about declining student competence in math as well. See "Schools going back to the basics, 'Pressure-free education' gets blame for sliding exam scores," *Japan Times*, September 9, 2010. The 2009 study comes from the Organisation for Economic Co-operation and Development, and was reported in the *National Post*, December 7, 2010.

Chapter 25

Most Canadians donate at least something to charity: according to the *CBC News*, 85 per cent made donations in 2006. The highest rate, 93 per cent, was in Newfoundland and Labrador; the lowest, 77 per cent, in British Columbia. But the bottom three-quarters of donors gave only 18 per cent of the donations. *CBC News* on-line, June 5, 2006.

Chapter 26

Statistics on foreign-born doctors in Canada are available from the Canadian Health Services Research Foundation. The figure of 22 per cent comes from an on-line article entitled "Mythbusters: Canadian doctors are leaving in droves for the United States." http://www.chsrf.ca/mythbusters/ html/myth29_e.php. Ignatieff's proposal was announced in a press release on July 22, 2010.

Chapter 29

Maclean's recently (November 10, 2010) carried an article suggesting that American attempts to limit Asian enrolment at their universities might divert the flow to Canada, making our universities "too Asian."

Chapter 32

In 2004, according to educationCanada.com, the average teacher in BC, the highest paid jurisdiction in Canada, earned a maximum of $56,700 with four years of education, and $70,700 with six years. The top salary in that province now is about $90,000.

Chapter 33

The figure of 80% of scientists is asserted by David Goodstein at http://www.its.caltech.edu/~dg/crunch_art.html.

Chapter 34
The lists of the councils' awards are available on-line.

Chapter 35
Shortage of spaces in the Greater Toronto Area: Ian D. Clark, "Challenges in university financing and accessibility in Ontario," Presentation to the Faculty of Arts and Sciences Town Hall, University of Toronto, January 28, 2009.

Chapter 36
School closures in Prince George, *CBC News* on-line, January 20, 2010.

Chapter 43
"What They're Reading on College Campuses," *The Chronicle of Higher Education*, January 20, 2010.

Chapter 46
Oliver Goldsmith (1730–74), *The Deserted Village* (1770).

Chapter 49
Study times: "Declining Study Time Signals Falling Standards, Report Says," *The Chronicle of Higher Education*, August 5, 2010.

Chapter 68
There is an organization for English sessionals in Canada, affiliated with the Association of Canadian College and University Teachers of English. An article entitled "The Sessional Situation" posted on its website in June 2010 has a great deal of information about English sessional instructors in Canada. http://www.accute.ca/sessionalreport.html

Chapter 73
The figure of 300 million was given in 2006 by Wu Qidi, a "senior Chinese education official." English.peopledaily.com, March 27, 2006. This includes people who have studied it even briefly. Other sources give different figures: *Newsweek International* for August 20–27, 2007 gives a figure of 175 million.

Chapter 74

For default rates on student loans, see http://www.hrsdc.gc.ca/eng/learning/canada_student_loan/Publications/annual_report/2004-2005/page08.shtml.

Chapter 76

Ed Dante, "The Shadow Scholar: The man who writes your students' papers tells his story," *The Chronicle of Higher Education*, November 12, 2010.

Chapter 79

Figures for fees tend to be elusive and hard to compare. The figure for Concordia is for tuition, but there are other compulsory per-credit fees—Student Service, Recreation & Athletics, Technology Infrastructure, and Copyright and Administrative fees. A more realistic figure is about $3,400 for the Montreal student, and $7,500 for the one from New Brunswick. The figures are available on the web from the individual universities. Statistics Canada reported that Quebec had the third-lowest university participation rate in Canada, while the president of McGill said it was the second-lowest. Professor Heather Munroe-Blum, "Universities and the future of Quebec: Comme les deux doigts de la main," Speech to the Canadian Club of Montreal, June 14, 2010.

Chapter 80

The percentage of students becoming Ontario Scholars is from Alan Slavin, "Has Ontario taught its high school students not to think? *University Affairs*, September 10, 2007.

Chapter 81

Figures for enrolment and degrees awarded by gender are available on-line from Statistics Canada. The historical statistic is from http://www.statcan.gc.ca/pub/11-516-x/sectionw/4147445-eng.htm#3. A table showing the number of women and men, full and part time, graduate and undergraduate, from 2005 to 2009, can be found at http://www.statcan.gc.ca/daily-quotidien/100714/t100714a1-eng.htm.

Chapter 84

University World News, April 12, 2009, quotes official Chinese sources on graduate unemployment. Figures for the number of Chinese universities and university students vary according to source. The figure of eight million students comes from Wang Huiyao, Director General of the Centre for Globalization in Beijing and Vice-chair of the China Talent Research Society under the Ministry of Human Resources, quoted in Yojana Sharma, "China: Ambitious 'innovation society' plan," *University World News*, November 15, 2010, available on-line. Figures for the number of Canadians with degrees come from *1961: Census of Canada* (1963) Table 102, and subsequent censuses.

Chapter 86

David Bercuson, Robert Bothwell, and J.L. Granatstein, *The Great Brain Robbery*. Toronto: McClelland and Stewart, 1984.

Chapter 96

Information on the Saskatchewan plan is available on-line at http://www.aeei.gov.sk.ca/grp.

Chapter 98

Figures for university endowments are widely available on-line. Toronto's are at http://www.finance.utoronto.ca/Assets.

Chapter 100

The source for the OECD figures is http://www.science.gc.ca/default.asp?lang=en&n=22BCE31A-1. For comparative faculty salaries, see http://www.cautbulletin.ca/en_article.asp?articleid=2741. On our "D" ranking, see http://www.conferenceboard.ca/hcp/details/ww.

Marquis Book Printing Inc.

Québec, Canada
2011